DICKENS'S LONDON

To Vera Saudková and Marianna Steiner

Dickens's London

Peter Clark

First published in 2012 by
The Armchair Traveller,
4 Cinnamon Row,
London SW11 3TW

This first paperback edition published in 2019

Copyright © Peter Clark 2012, 2019

Cartography produced by ML Design

Maps contain Ordnance Survey data © Crown copyright and database right 2011

A CIP catalogue for this book is available from the British Library

The moral right of the author has been asserted

ISBN 978-1-909961-67-8

Typeset in Garamond by MacGuru Ltd
Printed in the United Kingdom by TJ International Ltd

www.hauspublishing.com
@hauspublishing.com

Contents

St Luke's Church Chelsea, where Charles Dickens
married Catherine Hogarth in April 1836

To my grandson Thomas
in the confident expectation
that his generation will enjoy
the works of Charles Dickens as much
as the previous seven

Introduction

Wealth and beggary, vice and virtue, guilt and innocence, repletion and the direst hunger, all treading on each other and crowding together, are gathered round it. Draw but a little circle above the clustering housetops, and you shall have within its space everything, with its opposite extreme and contradiction, close beside.

Master Humphrey's Clock

THE CORE OF THIS BOOK consists of five walks around central London, noting places that have a reference either to the life of Charles Dickens or to his writings. I have referred not only to the fiction but also his journalism and his letters. These core sections are supplemented by passages on six places in London, but outside the central area, that have close connections with Dickens's life and work: Camden Town, Chelsea, Greenwich, Hampstead, Highgate and Limehouse. The net could have been cast wider. Chigwell with its public house celebrated in *Barnaby Rudge*; Shepherd's Bush, the location of a refuge for women who had fallen on bad times, set up by Dickens and Baroness Coutts; Richmond where Dickens loved to eat at the Star and Garter and where Mr Tupman of *Pickwick Papers* retired to live in lodgings; Hounslow, where at the Coach and Horses public house Bill Sikes and Oliver Twist paused on their way to the robbery at Chertsey; or Peckham where Dickens found a home for his intimate friend, Ellen Ternan, and her family.

In the course of researching and writing this book, it has turned out that not a lot of the fabric of the places and buildings familiar to Dickens has survived. We have to reconstruct in our minds a building that no longer exists and understand how it was seen and used by Dickens. Moreover we have to remember that his novels are fiction, not reportage or documentation. But such is the power of Dickens's fiction and impact on our imaginations that we have difficulty in separating fiction from fact. Earlier commentators had the same problem. As did Dickens himself: he would take people around parts of London and tell them just where some incident in his novels took place.

Robert Allbut wrote *London Rambles 'en Zigzag' with Charles Dickens* ten or so years after Dickens's death in 1870. It was a small brochure and was published in 1886 by Chapman and Hall (Dickens's own publisher) and went through several editions, was expanded and updated. As the brochure became a book, so it changed its name to *Rambles in Dickensland*. Its author was born Robert Allbut Gollop in Poole, Dorset, in 1832. Professionally he worked in a firm of travel agents. He was an avid Dickens reader from his youth and read many of them as they came out in monthly parts. He was a frequent contributor to *The Dickensian* and died in 1915. The undated edition I have worked from was published in about 1903 and includes not just London, but places – Rochester, Canterbury, Dover, Henley-on-Thames, East Anglia, Dorking and Portsmouth – that can be reached in a day's outing from the capital. The Midlands and Preston (now presumed to be Coketown in *Hard Times*) and northern Yorkshire (the site of Dotheboys Hall in *Nicholas Nickleby*) are excluded.

In the generation after the death of Charles Dickens many books were written on the places described or alluded to in Dickens's novels. Some had "tramp" or "ramble" in the title, and referred to visits to the places as "pilgrimages". Allbut's work was one of many such books.

Often the authors of these books located sites with precision,

Robert Allbut particularly so. There is no doubt that many locations described in Dickens's novels were based on places familiar to or remembered by Dickens. But there was always a limit. His son, Charles Dickens Junior, wrote in 1896 that it was true "that many of the places described in Charles Dickens's books were suggested by real localities or buildings, but the more the question comes to be examined, the more clear it is that all that was done with the prototype, was to use it as a painter or a sculptor uses a sketch, and that, under the hand of the writer and in the natural process of evolution, it has grown, in almost every case, into a finished picture, with few, if any, very salient points about it to render its origin unmistakable." He went on to quote approvingly from a review of one of those early books, *Bozland, Dickens' Places and People* by Percy Fitzgerald, published in 1895. The review said that Dickens "was not content simply to reproduce the places, persons, things that he had seen and known. He passed them through the crucible of his imagination, fused them, re-combined their elements, changed them into something richer and rarer, gave them forth as products of his art."

These observations could be further qualified. Sometimes Dickens used the names of real places and sites, and it is easy to locate them with precision. He also slightly disguised the names of other places, or gave them names that were not difficult to decode – such as Cloisterham for Rochester in *The Mystery of Edwin Drood*. At other times he avoided giving places names at all. In *The Old Curiosity Shop* we are given few hints about the journey through the Midlands taken by Little Nell and her Grandfather. It has been deduced that they passed through Buckinghamshire and that the walk through industrial England was from Birmingham to Wolverhampton and that they ended up at the village of Tong in Shropshire, but this is only based on what Dickens himself revealed. Indeed Dickens was so prolific in his journalism and in his correspondence that there are ample clues to infer what he had in mind. Even so there have been disputes about locations. Today it is accepted that Eatanswill in *Pickwick Papers* is Sudbury, Suffolk, and that Coketown in *Hard Times* is Preston, Lancashire. It was not always so. Early scholars of Dickens geography argued that Eatanswill was Ipswich and that Coketown was Manchester. Today's consensus is based on a reading of Dickens's letters and tracing his movements in the years before the writing of these novels.

But for London, Dickens was generally quite specific. He knew London intimately and there is rarely any ambiguity about locating sites he had in his mind when he was writing his fiction. Research in the last half century on the years from his residence as a child in London to his first publications has shown how vividly his observations were used for his fiction for the rest of his life. But in addition to being England's most popular and perhaps greatest novelist, Dickens was also a brilliant journalist. His extraordinary sensitivity to mood, place and people is transferred to his copious articles for the journals he edited, *Household Words* and *All the Year Round*. Journalism was often written at speed, for a deadline, but it is not too difficult to see how his articles were used for his fiction.

In the expanded volume by Robert Allbut I have used, an 1899 preface by Allbut notes how he had had to add to the earlier editions and also to revise paragraphs. This was because of what he called "the steady progress of Metropolitan improvements". He noted that, especially in the neighbourhood of The Strand and of Holborn, "many alterations have taken place, and another London is springing up around a younger generation, not known to Dickens". That was over a hundred years ago. Since then we have had two world wars, the second of which was particularly devastating to Dickens's London, and further "metropolitan improvements". Indeed in the last thirty years, the whole visual landscape of London – alongside many other major cities of the world – has undergone colossal changes, physical and demographic.

Massive transformations took place during Dickens's lifetime. At the beginning of the nineteenth century streets were narrow and crowded, and in many parts there were horrendously squalid slums. Throughout the century whole areas were cleared up. New roads destroyed slums and provided more direct access to different parts of the city: Queen Victoria Street, New Oxford Street, Victoria Street, Northumberland Avenue, Charing Cross Road, Southwark Street. Bridges across the Thames were widened or made more accessible with the removal of tolls. Above all the railways revolutionised the urban geography. Railway termini provided new focal points for the city.

In the last century some of the physical changes have been so taken for granted that it is hard to imagine London without them. Let us consider three, in order of construction – Trafalgar Square, the Embankment and Holborn Viaduct.

Trafalgar Square was built in the 1820s ostensibly to celebrate the victory of Nelson over the French. But it was also built with an eye to social control. Broad roads led to the square, facilitating the movement of troops. It must be remembered that the years after the Napoleonic Wars were years of unrest. Comfortable classes felt threatened. Paradoxically, the square has in the last century become a focus of agitation, usually against policies supported by those comfortable classes.

Dickens during his most sensitive, vulnerable and impressionable years – when he was working at the blacking factory at a spot between The Strand and the river Thames – knew the area of Trafalgar Square and the Embankment before the improvements. He wandered around the area, was familiar with the inns and alleyways, the river bank and the jetties. Much of what he knew was swept away, first by the building of Trafalgar Square, secondly by the construction of the Embankment in the 1860s. It has to be borne in mind that The Strand was once literally just that, a strand, a beach.

There were houses on the river side of the street, including palaces like the Savoy and Somerset House that would have had jetties and piers directly on to the river. What is now Victoria Embankment Gardens was, until the building of that Embankment, subject to tidal flooding.

A mile or so to the north is Holborn. The suffix *born* is the same as "burn", a Celtic word meaning river. The old parish of Holborn was built on both sides of a valley, along which flowed the River Fleet. Holborn Viaduct was built in 1865, together with the road to the west, New Oxford Street, in order to facilitate access between the commercial centre of the City of London and Oxford Street, a smart residential and consumer servicing area. Before the building of the viaduct, travellers along the east-west axis had to go down a sharp and relatively steep gradient to the valley of the Fleet and then up again. The Fleet here was in the early nineteenth century a noisome ditch, with a notorious prison to the south. Grim hovels and streets bordered the stream. This was the Fagin country of Snow Hill and Field Lane. All these slums were swept away with the improvements of the 1860s. The name of Field Lane disappeared but Snow Hill has been retained.

During the nineteenth century London also expanded to meet the needs of a huge immigration of people from the rural areas. It is sometimes useful to see nineteenth century London analogous to a late twentieth century Third World city. In the generation between the 1820s and the 1850s, the period of Dickens's maturing and of his most intensive creativity, the population of London rose from one and a half million to two and a half million – sixty per cent. Unlike twentieth-century population increases it was not as a result of improved health services and a lower death rate. Much was a consequence of immigration from rural England. It means that by the 1850s a large proportion of Londoners were born outside the capital. Dickens himself was a migrant from the English provinces. And he was able to describe the world and the values of individuals who were outside an inherited social pattern, had to live on their wits and establish their own identity – he was indeed a supreme example of such individuals.

In the 1840s it was still possible to get to know all of built up London on foot. In the 1690s King William III had built Kensington Palace as a rural retreat. One hundred and fifty years later it was still fairly rural. To the east were Kensington Gardens and Hyde Park. To the west the village of Kensington. To the north Paddington was on the edge of the urban area. Warwick Avenue was being laid out for construction. There was ribbon development along Edgware Road as far as the village of Kilburn, but the Swiss Cottage Tavern was surrounded by fields. Belsize Park was a park and Primrose Hill a hill. There were few buildings north of Regent's Park. Railway development in the previous decade – noted in *Dombey and Son* – was transforming Camden Town, where Dickens spent some of his childhood, but Regent's Canal meandered east to west with gardens to the north. To the north of the present Euston Road was a smart newly planned suburb, Somers Town, but the King's Cross/ St Pancras railway complex had not been built. Some squalid streets and a gas works occupied that site. The new suburb of Pentonville had recently extended the city to the north, joining the city with the village of Islington. To the north open land separated the Regent's Canal from the village of Hackney. Victoria Park had already been designed and opened for the grimmer suburbs of Bethnal Green and Globe Town. Then to the south Bromley New Town was being planned, but otherwise between the ribbon development of Mile End Road and Commercial Road there was, apart from a cemetery, a common and open land. South of Commercial Road the Docks had seen huge development in the previous decade, parallel to the development of large steam-powered ships. The Isle of Dogs was largely marshy land below sea level, Greenwich had a separate identity, and Deptford had for long been a well-established port and town. Away from the river, what is now Evelyn Street went through open country from Rotherhithe to Deptford. Walworth, the south-eastern part of Southwark was built up, as were the areas of Newington and Lambeth. North of the river, outer Westminster was marked by the penitentiary in Millbank and the Bridewell, another disciplinary detention centre, but there was uninterrupted, albeit modern, building beginning to stretch to the village of Chelsea. Earl's Court was surrounded by open country but the area between the Fulham Road and Kensington was about to be urbanised.

In the thirty years after the 1840s London lost its eighteenth century character. Public transport, the underground and the railways, led to people moving out to the suburbs. Central London became emptier, especially at night. It was a city primarily for work. There was a social cantonisation. At the beginning of the century smart quarters were close to the slums. Legal London was cheek by jowl with criminal London. But with affordable public transport people no longer walked up to ten miles a day from their homes to their places of work. They were able to live further away. Suburbs were born. In the year of Dickens's death London – with its wide streets, neo-Gothic buildings and advertisement hoardings – is recognisable to us today, in a way the narrow streets and close-packed communities of the eighteenth-century city is not.

The changes of the last century and a half have not only been physical. There have also been seismic social changes. The greatest changes have been in Southwark, Bermondsey, and the East End of Wapping and Limehouse. Former slums have been replaced by properties that fetch the highest of prices. Sometimes an old working man's pub has survived, looking like a man in overalls who has strayed into a smart reception. But it is still possible to read the social archaeology of a district.

One of the biggest social changes since Dickens's time has

been the internationalisation of the city. Today it is reckoned that over three hundred languages are spoken by the children at inner London schools. Dickens recorded foreigners' London – French, Spanish and Italian immigrants; and Jews, bad like Fagin in *Oliver Twist*, and good like Mr Riah in *Our Mutual Friend*. But they are socially outsiders. Today the social and racial mix in inner London would have been inconceivable in Dickens's time. Dickens had very racist views. Rarely does anyone from outside Europe appear in his novels. One exception is the "Native" servant of Major Bagstock in *Dombey and Son*. But he is a comic figure, with no inner life; indeed he does not even have the dignity of a name. In *The Mystery of Edwin Drood* there is described a visit to an opium smokers' den, where we meet a sleeping Chinaman and Lascar. But there was not yet any Chinatown.

Parts of London have not changed socially. Dickens was not assured in writing about the wealthier or more influential classes, especially in the earlier novels. Sir Mulberry Hawk and Lord Frederick Verisopht in *Nicholas Nickleby* are caricatures. As is Sir Leicester Dedlock in *Bleak House*. Lady Dedlock less so. But the geography of upper class London has not changed: the squares of Mayfair and Belgravia are still the homes of the very rich, albeit an international plutocracy. In Dickens's time these areas provided the homes of the Merdles in *Little Dorrit* and the Veneerings in *Our Mutual Friend*.

Dickens was most familiar with the areas from Camden Town to the river, with Southwark and the City. But his knowledge of the areas beyond these was phenomenal. As one friend observed, "I thought I knew something of the town, but after a little talk with Dickens I found I knew nothing. He knew it all from Bow to Brentford." George Augustus Sala, son of an Italian immigrant, worked with Dickens on *Household Words* and *All the Year Round*. He was amazed at Dickens's range of contacts. Everybody seemed to know him: "... the omnibus conductors knew him, the street boys knew him ... he would turn up in the oddest places, and in the most inclement of weather ... he knew all about the backstreets behind Holborn, the courts and alleys of the Borough, the shabby sidling streets of the remoter suburbs, the crooked little alleys of the City, the dank and oozy wharfs of the water-side. He was at home in the lodging houses, station-houses, cottages, hovels, Cheap Jacks' caravans, workhouses, prisons, school-rooms, chandlers' shops, back attics, barbers' shops, areas, back yards, dark entries, public-houses, rag-shops, police-courts, and markets in poor neighbourhoods." His powers of observation and memory – and his skill and speed at transforming observations into prose – have made his novels, journalism and correspondence a unique source of information on the social history of London.

He described his methods to an American admirer, G D Carrow, who reports Dickens as saying that he used to walk around the seedier parts of London, **preserving an air of preoccupation, and affecting as near as possible the ways of a collector of house rents or of a physician going his rounds. When any scene of especial interest attracted my notice I usually halted at a crossing as if waiting for a conveyance or as if undecided which way to go. Or else I would stop and purchase some trifle, chatting with the vendor and taking my time for making a selection, or would order a glass of half-and-half, wait for the froth to subside, and then consume an hour in sipping it to the bottom.**

As a boy, he walked the three miles from Camden Town to The Strand every day. This was not unusual. In his novels he had people coming to work in a similar way over comparable distances. In *A Christmas Carol* Bob Cratchit walks each day from Camden Town to the City. In *Great Expectations*, Wemmick, John Jaggers's clerk, walks to and from Walworth. And in *Our Mutual Friend* Reginald Wilfer walks into central London from Holloway, and back at night.

During his meal breaks at the factory on the approximate site of which stands Charing Cross station, he wandered along the river bank or inland, in parts that were completely altered by the improvements.

But he was not nostalgic. Central London absorbed his energies from the time he gazed at the city from the semi-rural Camden Town which was his first home after Kent. He would look at London from afar: the view **over the dust heaps and dock-leaves and fields ... at the cupola of St Paul's looming through the smoke, was a treat that served for hours of vague reflection afterwards.**

His powers of observation were not limited to the physical environment nor to the range of dialects overheard. He had an acute sense of place and social hierarchy. For example, in *Nicholas Nickleby*, he writes of Cadogan Place, the home of the pretentious Mrs Witterly: **It is in Sloane Street, but not of it. The people in Cadogan Place look down upon Sloane Street and think Brompton low. They affect fashion too, and wonder where the New Road is. Not that they claim to be on precisely the same footing as the high folks of Belgrave Square and Grosvenor Place, but that they stand with reference to them, rather in the light of those illegitimate children of the great who are content to boast of their connections, although their connections disavow them.**

That was when he was in his twenties. Thirty years later he was rubbing shoulders with people unquestionably at the top of the social tree. In March 1870 he had an audience with Queen Victoria. In spite of frailty, he complied with protocol by standing up all the time. He was already a close friend of the aristocratic Bulwer Lytton and a regular visitor to his country house, Knebworth, in Hertfordshire. He sent one of his sons to Eton College. And in the last few weeks of his life he had breakfast with the Prime Minister, W E Gladstone, dined with the head of the United States Embassy, with the former and future Prime Minister (and fellow-novelist)

Benjamin Disraeli, and had dinner with Monckton Milnes, Lord Houghton, to meet the Prince of Wales.

Most of his earlier fiction was located in the London of his childhood and he drew on adolescent memories, observations and experiences. In his early novels London was a kind of addictive drug. When he started living abroad for months at a time, he would miss the variety and stimulus of the city. In 1846 he took a villa in Lausanne, Switzerland, where he wrote much of *Dombey and Son*. **For a week or a fortnight I can write prodigiously in a retired place,** he wrote. **But the toil and labour of writing, day after day, without that magic lantern is IMMENSE!!**

But as he came to maturity, prosperity and celebrity he expressed mixed feelings, and even some detachment from the city. **A city of Devils,** he called it. **London is a vile place,** he wrote to Bulwer Lytton in 1850, **I sincerely believe. I have never taken kindly to it since I lived abroad. Whenever I come back from the Country now, and see that great heavy canopy lowering over the housetops, I wonder what on earth I do here, except on obligation.** It was not only in private correspondence that he berated London. In an article, reprinted in *The Uncommercial Traveller*, he wrote that the **shabbiness of our English capital, as compared with Paris, Bordeaux, Frankfort, Milan, Geneva – almost any important town on the continent of Europe – I find very striking after an absence of any duration in foreign parts. London is shabby in contrast with Edinburgh, with Aberdeen, with Exeter, with Liverpool, with a bright little town like Bury St Edmunds. London is shabby in contrast with New York, with Boston, with Philadelphia.** Indeed it was his travel and residence abroad that gave him detachment. He was impressed by the efficiency and broad streets of Paris, by the readiness to oblige the visitor. He cruelly and sarcastically contrasts the quality of food and the service at a restaurant at a French railway station with what is available at the British equivalent. In the 1850s he wrote to his not yet estranged wife, **the streets are hideous to behold, and the ugliness of London is quite astonishing.** And in his last novel, *The Mystery of Edwin Drood*, he saw London as full of melancholy streets in a penitential garb of soot. There were **deserts of gritty streets, where many people crowded at the corners of courts and bye-ways, to get some air. And where many other people walked with a miserably monotonous noise of shuffling feet on hot paving-stones, and where all the people and all their surroundings were so gritty and so shabby.**

Dickens had a nervous restlessness when in London. Although he lived in three homes for substantial periods, each one more spacious than the previous, he was never attached to them as he became attached to Gad's Hill Place, near Rochester in Kent. He was only in Doughty Street for three years. The house at Devonshire Terrace, where he lived for twelve years, was the place of his greatest activity. Tavistock House, which he occupied for nine years, was perhaps too closely associated with the breakdown of his marriage. After he left Tavistock House he had bachelor quarters in the offices of *All the Year Round* off The Strand. But otherwise he rented a different house almost every year, ostensibly for his family. He also took lodgings in Peckham to be near Ellen Ternan and her family. But in his latter years he was most at ease with himself either at Gad's Hill Place or at houses he rented in France.

It is recommended that people who wish to follow a walk take their time – perhaps devote a day to each walk. Although the focus is on Dickens's London, the walks pass by much else of historic, social and literary interest.

It is also recommended that they take with them a good London road atlas, as well as a waterproof. The walks all pass by restaurants of every kind and cuisine, catering for all budgets. And there are also the taverns and public houses associated with Dickens and his work that provide food from a sandwich to a slap-up meal.

The Wellington Street offices of *All the Year Round*

From Trafalgar Square to Lincoln's Inn Fields

The first walk covers the area Dickens got to know when he worked at the blacking factory and fictionalised in **David Copperfield.** *We pass by sites associated with the life and work around The Strand and Covent Garden.*

T RAFALGAR SQUARE with its soaring Nelson's Column is one of the most iconic sites of London. But when Dickens was a lad, the area was quite different. There was no Square, no Column. In those days three major roads converged – Cockspur Street from the west, The Strand from the east and Whitehall from the south. The London palace of the Dukes of Northumberland, with extensive gardens, occupied the area to the south east. Palace and gardens made way for Northumberland Avenue in the 1870s. There was no Charing Cross Road: that came in the 1880s. Tucked away on St Martin's Lane was the church of St Martin-in-the-Fields, the only building in the area that predates the design in the 1820s of Trafalgar Square, to commemorate Britain's greatest sailor and his battle of Trafalgar. The construction of Trafalgar Square brought out the church's spectacular position. The present church was designed by James Gibbs in the 1720s although a church has been on the site

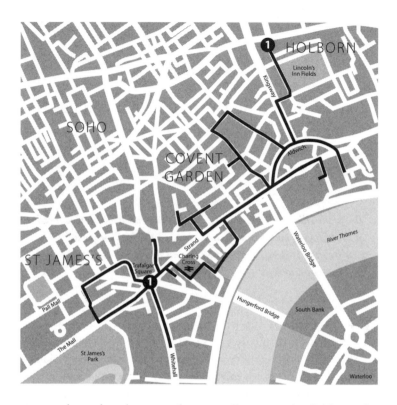

since early medieval times, when it really was in the fields. In the
time of Dickens's childhood, the area around St Martin's church was
full of what a later generation would call fast food stalls and was
known as "Porridge Island". It was opposite the church that David
Copperfield met Mr Peggotty by chance before they both adjourned
to the Golden Cross Hotel.

Dickens knew the area intimately before the changes and
expressed regret for the changes. (**I particularly observed the sin-
gularity of His Majesty's calling** *that* **an improvement,** he wrote
in 1851. And in a paper, published in *The Uncommercial Traveller* he

wrote of **the abortive ugliness of Trafalgar Square set against the gallant beauty of the Place de la Concorde.**)

To the west of the Square is Admiralty Arch which leads into the Mall, the grand avenue leading to Buckingham Palace. King William IV, who was on the throne when Dickens's first works were published, was the first monarch to turn what had been his mother's home, Buckingham House, into the home of the monarch and Buckingham Palace. Refurbishments were incomplete when he died in 1837 but his successor, his niece, Queen Victoria, established it as the London residence of the British monarch. She was a great admirer of Dickens's works and honoured him by granting him an audience at Buckingham Palace a few months before he died in the spring of 1870. It was to thank him for some photographs of American Civil War battlefields he had sent her at her request. Protocol required that he remain standing in the presence of Her Majesty, and he stood for an hour and a half, quite an ordeal for him on account of a swollen foot. He thought **she was strangely shy … and like a girl in manner … but with a girlish sort of timidity which was very engaging.**

North of the Mall is Clubland. The Athenaeum is at the corner of Pall Mall and Waterloo Place. Dickens was elected to this club in 1838 at the same time as Charles Darwin. (Dickens was also a member of the Garrick Club.) He used to have his lunch at a table in the window, facing the United Services Club, now occupied by the Institute of Directors. The foyer of the Athenaeum witnessed the scene of a reconciliation of Dickens and his contemporary, W M Thackeray. Dickens was less than one year younger than Thackeray and achieved fame first. Both were admirers of the other's work and became friends, although they were very different. Thackeray came from a wealthy family that had made money in trade in India. He went to the major public school, Charterhouse, and on to Trinity College, Cambridge. There was always an assured social confidence about him. But when Dickens split with his wife and befriended the actress, Ellen Ternan, there were rumours that Dickens was having an affair with his sister-in-law, Georgina. Thackeray is reported to have denied this, saying, "It's with an actress." Dickens was acutely sensitive to such rumours and for several years Dickens and Thackeray were not on speaking terms. But in 1863 both perchance bumped into each other at the Athenaeum. One story has it that Dickens made the first move. **"Thackeray, have you been ill?"** he asked. They both shook hands and felt better for it. "I am glad I have done this," Thackeray is reported to have said. Within a month he was dead, and Dickens wrote a generous tribute of the other novelist.

The Golden Cross was the focal point of the junction of the three roads. This was one of the great coaching houses of the city. Just as London today has a number of terminal railway stations each of which serves one part of the country so it was, to some extent, with the great coaching houses. The Angel at Islington was the coaching inn for Yorkshire – Nicholas Nickleby set off from here to accompany Wackford Squeers to Greta Bridge. From The Bell at Whitechapel, passengers set off for East Anglia, as Mr Pickwick and his companions did, en route for Ipswich. For Bath and the west, one set from the White Horse Cellar at the junction of Dover Street and Piccadilly. (The Bath coach was owned by a man called Moses Pickwick.) And for travellers to and from the south of England, the special inn was The White Hart, Southwark, where Mr Pickwick and Sam Weller first met. But the Golden Cross was the starting point for coaches to destinations all over England, though in the novels of Dickens it was the Kent destinations for which it was most celebrated, especially to Rochester and Canterbury.

From the Golden Cross, on 13 May 1827, Mr Samuel Pickwick and his three fellow-members of the Pickwick Club – Alfred Snodgrass, Tracy Tupman and Nathaniel Winkle – set off on their Kentish travels in the company of Alfred Jingle. A dangerously low archway used to lead into a courtyard. Jingle told the story of how **other day – five children – mother – tall lady, eating sandwiches – forgot the arch – crash – knock – children look round – mother's head off – sandwich in her hand – no mouth to put it in – head of family off – shocking – shocking.**

The Golden Cross Hotel of the time of Pickwick used to occupy the area north of the present Trafalgar Square. The cross probably referred to the Eleanor Cross, erected in memory of the wife of King Edward I, who reigned from 1272 to 1307. The cross was originally located at the point currently occupied by the statue of King Charles I. It was known as Charing Cross and it has been romantically suggested that Charing was a corruption of the French, *chère reine*, dear queen, but the name of Charing is much older. The present cross outside Charing Cross Station was constructed in 1865.

Although there were inns of this name going back to the seventeenth century, the building that Dickens knew and referred to in *Pickwick Papers* was built in 1811 in the Gothic style. It did not last long. It has been reckoned that the front gateway, immortalised by the words of Alfred Jingle, was roughly on the site of one of the lions below Nelson's Column, with the stable yard to the north. When Trafalgar Square was designed in 1829 the Gothic Golden Cross was demolished and rebuilt in the area between Trafalgar Square and where Duncannon Street now is. That hotel lasted until 1931 to make way for South Africa House.

At the Golden Cross Hotel, David Copperfield, after his education at Dr Strong's in Canterbury, met up with his old school friend, the dangerous and worldly James Steerforth.

Whitehall leads out of Trafalgar Square to the south, to Westminster. One of the first buildings on the left is the architecturally perfect Banqueting Hall, designed by in Inigo Jones between 1619 and 1622, as part of the royal Whitehall Palace. From a room on the first floor King Charles I stepped out to his execution block. Or, as

Mr Jingle in *Pickwick Papers* said, **"Looking at Whitehall, Sir – fine place – little window – somebody else's head off there, eh, Sir? – he didn't keep a sharp look out either – eh, Sir, eh?"**

To the north of Trafalgar Square adjacent to the National Gallery is the National Portrait Gallery. In a room dedicated to Victorian writers is a painting of Dickens by his friend, Daniel Maclise, in 1839, when Dickens was twenty-seven, at the height of his early fame. George Eliot described the portrait as "keepsakey". Dickens is at a desk, his left hand awkwardly on a manuscript. His bright eyes look out, wide open and receptive to all he saw. His clothes are elegant and slightly flashy, his shoes highly polished. His studied neatness shines out. He always paid attention to his appearance, just as he was always tidy and punctual. His legs are crossed as if he was not entirely at ease.

If we turn into The Strand, before Charing Cross Station, some steps and a ramp between two shops take us down into Craven Street, which runs down to Northumberland Avenue. In the nineteenth century the street was full of boarding houses, providing a service for passengers who arrived by coach at the Golden Cross or, after the station was built in 1865, by train. Number 39, on the eastern side, was the home of Mr Brownlow in *Oliver Twist*, after he moved away from Pentonville. Four doors further down is the house that was the home of Benjamin Franklin when he lived in London. It is now a museum. If we go through the Arches underneath the station we come to Villiers Street. To the right is Hungerford Bridge for the railway with pedestrian crossings on either side.

Hungerford Bridge is all that is left of the name of an area called after a Somerset family that owned Farleigh Hungerford Castle south-east of Bath. Charing Cross Station was built on the site of Hungerford Market. Dickens worked at a factory that manufactured blacking here in 1824. The factory belonged to a relative, James Lamert, and Dickens was paid six or seven shillings a week – not a bad salary then for a boy of twelve. (Grown men with families often had to manage on less.) His task was to put covers on to pots of paste-blacking and label them. It was humiliating work and though he rarely spoke openly about it he remembered the experience with bitterness for the rest of his life, **servitude**, he called it. Although the experience lasted under six months, nothing affected him so much. He had come to London after five happy years in Chatham, where he had discovered reading, and enjoyed the city of Rochester and the countryside around. The family moved to London when Charles's father, John Dickens, was given a job at Somerset House. But soon after he started at the factory John was arrested for debt and incarcerated at the Marshalsea Prison in Southwark. The family needed the money. Some commentators suggest that the experience was central to much of his creativity. He empathised with neglected children, caught in what would later be called a cycle of deprivation. He had been lucky enough to escape because of his extraordinary talents – of which, without false modesty, he was fully aware. Thousands, millions of others were sucked down into humiliating poverty. At the age of twelve he was sensitive and observant and impressions remained with him with stark clarity for the rest of his life.

Though unwilling to talk about these experiences, he did open up to his friend and biographer, John Forster, and recorded his bitterness in an autobiographical manuscript he gave to Forster. But he used the memory in the account of David Copperfield doing similar work, thanks to his brutal stepfather, for the firm of Murdstone and Grinby. David's factory was further downstream, at Blackfriars. The site of Dickens's factory has been replaced by the railway. Dickens remembered the place as **a crazy, tumble-down old house, abutting, of course, on the river, and literally overrun with rats. Its wainscotted rooms and its rotten floors and staircase, and the old grey rats swarming down in the cellars, and the sound of their** squeaking and scuffling coming up the stairs at all times, and the dirt and decay of the place, rise up vividly before me, as if I were there again.

He was living at Camden Town when he started and would walk the three miles there and back each day. This was not unusual. Thirty years later it was reckoned that 400,000 regularly walked into the City every day. Dickens's youthful walks were a good preparation for his habit throughout his life of energetic urban walking. He worked here ten hours a day with breaks for lunch at twelve and an afternoon break for tea.

When Dickens was working here there was no Embankment. The Strand was so named because it was the upper limit of the strand, or beach, of the tidal river Thames. The Strand was the main road from the city of London to the royal and official establishments of Westminster and Whitehall. In late medieval and Tudor times the eastern side of the The Strand was flanked by mansions belonging to major aristocrats and leading churchmen. Their estates faced the river and used to have jetties for their craft. Travel by the river until the nineteenth century was preferable, more efficient and cleaner than travel on land. The Watergate, built in 1626, marked the access for people disembarking and entering the gardens of one of these estates, that belonging to John Villiers, Duke of Buckingham, a favourite of King Charles I. The property had earlier belonged to the Archbishops of York. Hence the perpetuation of their names in the streets in the area.

The Victoria Embankment was built in the 1860s, although there had been proposals for such a project from as early as the seventeenth century. But the huge increase in London's population in the first half of the nineteenth century led to acute problems of sewage: the basically medieval system could not cope. Most sewage went directly or indirectly into the river Thames – there were sixty outlets into the river. London, especially in the warm summer of

1858, suffered from what was known as "The Great Stink". A Metropolitan Board of Works had been set up and its inspirational engineer, Joseph Bazalgette, had the idea of a huge sewage pipe parallel to the river, that would collect much of the sewage of the city north of the river and take it far away towards the Thames Estuary. So the tidal area was reclaimed, the river became enclosed and a giant pipe was constructed under the road. At the same time the underground line – now the District and Circle Line – was built in another tunnel parallel to the sewer and the river. And above were built the attractive gardens. These transformations took place during Dickens's lifetime. The gardens were opened by the Prince of Wales in July 1870 just one month after Dickens's death.

But Dickens, when he worked at the factory, got to know these quarters, with the wharves and squalid buildings, soon to be swept away. In later years the painful memories had made it impossible for him to return there until Hungerford Market was pulled down and the Hungerford Stairs destroyed. But he was able to reproduce aspects of the area in *David Copperfield*. In this novel Mr Peggotty spent a night over a chandler's shop in Hungerford Market, and when David Copperfield's aunt, Betsey Trotwood, came to London, her crazed companion, Mr Dick, occupied Peggotty's bedroom. It was very small and the landlady, Mrs Crupp, assured him that there was not enough room to swing a cat in it ... **but, as Mr Dick justly observed, "You know, Trotwood, I don't want to swing a cat. I never do swing a cat".** And the Micawber family had lodgings in this area just before they departed for Australia, **in a dirty, tumbledown public-house ... whose protruding wooden rooms overhung the river.** The darker aspects of the area have not entirely disappeared. Visitors to the outdoor seating of the bars by the gardens are reminded of pickpockets and are advised to thwart casual thieves by using "the bag hooks under the tables".

A little further downstream is what used to be the Adelphi. In the eighteenth century, the three Adam brothers, in Greek *adelphoi*, built a large grand riverside complex, with luxurious housing facing the river, and warehouses underneath. Access to them was by arches that were on the beach, as it were, of the river. Subsidiary streets running up to The Strand are all that are left of this ambitious project that could have rivalled Nash's Regent's Park or the Royal Crescent at Bath. It was never a success. Bureaucratic obstruction, aesthetic lack of interest, decay. The central block was ultimately demolished in 1936 and a graceless office block, the New Adelphi, constructed in its place. But when Dickens was a lad, he found it all alluring. His alter ego, David Copperfield, loved the area: **I was fond of wandering about the Adelphi, because it was a mysterious place, with those dark arches. I see myself emerging one evening from one of these arches, on a little public-house, close to the river, with an open space before it, where some coal-heavers were dancing.**

Away from the river the building on the northern corner of John Adam Street and Adam Street is the site of Osborne's Hotel, where, in *Pickwick Papers*, Mr Wardle, accompanied by his daughter, Emily, and the Fat Boy, Joe, stayed after Mr Pickwick was released from the Fleet Prison. Joe also discreetly observed Mr Snodgrass calling on his lady friend at this hotel.

Nearer the river – obviously before the building of the Embankment and the Victoria Embankment Gardens – there used to be a tavern, where Martin Chuzzlewit stayed on his arrival in London. Here he was visited by his faithful friend, Mark Tapley.

Another tavern, to the north-east of the Adelphi, was the Fox-under-the-Hill. It stood on the riverside, and could be approached from Ivy Bridge Lane, now the entry to the service area of the Shell-Mex House, built (in 1931–32) on the site of the Hotel Cecil which, in its time – 1885 – was the largest hotel in Europe. The developer of the Hotel, Jabez Balfour, ended up in prison for fraud. Dickens used to visit the Fox-under-the-Hill after work at the blacking factory and, like David Copperfield, watch coal-heavers dancing and the half-penny boats setting off on the river. Steamers used to ply from here to London Bridge, fare one half penny.

In *Martin Chuzzlewit* he described what could be seen here. **Little steamboats dashed up and down the stream incessantly. Tiers upon tiers of vessels, scores of masts, labyrinths of tackle, idle sails, splashing oars, gliding row-boats, lumbering barges, sunken piles with ugly lodging for the water-rat within their mud-discoloured nooks; church steeples, warehouses, house roofs, arches, bridges, men and women, children, casks, cranes, boxes, horses, coaches, idlers and hard labourers – they were all jumbled up together.**

And in *Little Dorrit*, published in 1857, Dickens reflected on the changes of the previous thirty years. **At that time the contrast was far greater; there being no small steam-boats on the river, no landing places but slippery wooden stairs and foot-causeways, no railroad on the opposite bank, no hanging bridge or fish market near at hand, no traffic on the nearest bridge of stone, nothing moving on the stream but watermen's wherries and coal-lighters. Long and black tiers of the latter moored fast in the mud as if they were never to move again, made the shore funereal and silent after dark; and kept what little water-movement there was, far out towards mid-stream.**

The next bridge downstream is Waterloo Bridge. The present bridge was built between 1937 and 1942, but its predecessor was built towards the end of the Napoleonic Wars. At first it was called the Strand Bridge but acquired its present name just one year after the Battle of Waterloo. In the middle of the nineteenth century it was a favourite bridge for suicides. In 1853 Dickens wrote an article for *Household Words* about a night he spent with the Thames River Police. **"If people jump off straight forward from the middle of the parapet of the bays of the bridge,"** explained one of Dickens's informants, "they are seldom killed by drowning, but are smashed, poor things; that's what *they* are; they dash themselves on the buttress of the bridge. But you jump off from the side of the bay, and you'll tumble, true, into the stream under the arch. What you have got to do, is to mind how you jump in! There was poor Tom Steele from Dublin. Didn't dive! Bless you, didn't dive at all! Fell down so flat into the water, that he broke his breast-bone, and lived two days!" People preferred to commit suicide from the southern side of the bridge, Dickens learnt.

A second blacking factory belonged to James Lamert in Chandos Place, parallel to and north of The Strand. The young Dickens and his fellow workers – including one called Bob Fagin – left the rat-infested warehouse by the river to work here. This can be reached by returning to The Strand, crossing over and walking up Bedford Street. This second factory is on the left at the junction with Chandos Place. The factory was pulled down in 1889, to be replaced by the curious red brick store, built in an Italian Renaissance revival style, looking like a parody of a Pall Mall Club. A plaque high up on the wall records that Charles Dickens worked here from 1824 to 1825. Dickens and his fellow-workers toiled by a window and Dickens was further humiliated by being the object of public curiosity as people stared in. Again the humiliation of this work remained with Dickens all his life. There was a smell of cement coming from the warehouse and when in later years he passed this way he would cross the road to avoid the smell.

A happier Dickens association can be found round the corner in Maiden Lane: Rules Restaurant. Founded in 1798 it is London's oldest restaurant. Dickens, in his prosperity, was a regular guest and there is a Dickens Room with playbills of his own productions and other memorabilia.

Doubling back westward along Chandos Place, Bedfordbury leads off to the north to New Row and, to the right, King Street. The

Peabody Buildings on the right – the result of the work of George Peabody, the Baltimore-born philanthropist – were built in the 1870s, replacing a jungle of old tenement buildings. Robert Allbut locates Tom-All-Alone's, home of poor Jo, the crossing-sweeper in *Bleak House*, here. Its approach was grim: **Mr Snagsby passes along the middle of a villainous street, undrained, unventilated, deep in black mud and corrupt water – though the roads are dry elsewhere – and reeking with such smells and sights that he, who has lived in London all his life, can scarce believe his senses.** Others have sited Tom-All-Alone's at the burial ground attached to the church of St Mary-le-Grand in Russell Street. But it is more probable that Tom-All-Alone's existed only in his imagination, for Dickens was usually quite specific about locations in *Bleak House*. The site epitomised macabre grimness – a place crammed with **heaps of dishonoured graves and stones, hemmed in by filthy houses ... on whose walls a thick humidity broke out like a disease.** He may have used the term from a place with that name in the Chatham of his boyhood. This Tom-All-Alone's was named after an eccentric recluse called Thomas Clark.

Back on The Strand, somewhere around the present Savoy Hotel, lived Miss La Creevy of *Nicholas Nickleby*. Ralph Nickleby came here, stopping ... **at a private door, about halfway down that crowded thoroughfare** [The Strand]. Miss La Creevy was based, perhaps, on a sister of Dickens's mother. Further along The Strand on the right is Somerset House, where Dickens's father worked for a while in the Navy Pay Office.

The present palatial building is the most outstanding public building in the capital. The land here between The Strand and the river was in medieval times the property of the Bishop of Chester. King Henry VIII seized the estate and handed it over to one of his "new men", Edward Seymour. The King married Jane Seymour, Edward's sister. She was the mother of King Henry VIII's immediate successor, the boy, King Edward VI. Edward Seymour, as the King's uncle and with the title of Lord Protector, became the most powerful man in the land. The young King made his uncle Duke of Somerset. The Duke cleared the land of religious buildings for his new palace. Unfortunately he was impeached and died before it was finished. The property reverted to the Crown and it was a royal palace for two centuries.

When in the 1770s King George III moved to Buckingham House (later Buckingham Palace), which then belonged to his wife, the present building was erected to house learned societies that were also under royal patronage and some government offices, including the Navy Board. The offices were near the river, from where it was easy to travel to the dockyards of Greenwich and Deptford. The magnificence of the building – Sir William Chambers was the architect – reflected the importance and grandeur of the navy. The Navy Board – where John Dickens worked – was located on the west side of the southern wing. This part was damaged in the Second World War.

In the twenty-first century the building has been transformed to become a centre of art, with galleries and a museum. It is now one of the capital's major cultural centres.

On the opposite side of The Strand in the 1830s were the offices of the newspaper, *Morning Chronicle*. Dickens himself worked for this paper when he was twenty and wrote his first reports for it. As a journalist he was sent on assignments around southern England, thereby acquiring a detailed knowledge of people and places. In the middle of the road is the church of St Mary-le-Strand. The church was designed in the early eighteenth century by James Gibbs, the architect of the church of St Martin-in-the-Fields. Thomas à Becket, the murdered twelfth-century Archbishop of Canterbury, was once rector here. This is where Dickens's parents were married in 1809. This church was selected because John Dickens was working close by at Somerset House, but after the wedding the couple moved to

Portsmouth, to the house in Mile End Terrace where Dickens was born three years later.

To the north of The Strand is Wellington Street North. At number 16 is a huge block housing the Indigo restaurant. But in 1850 it was a building that was **exceedingly pretty with the bowed front, the bow reaching up for two stories, each giving a flood of light.** These used to be the office of *Household Words*, the monthly magazine founded in 1850 to absorb some of Dickens's superabundant energies. He used to arrive at the office at eight in the morning and dictate for three hours, striding up and down, often combing his hair at the same time, a public habit that offended the Americans on his first visit to the United States. A few years later the offices were moved to number 26, which became the offices of *All the Year Round*, another of his magazines. This magazine developed young men of talent who referred to Dickens as "The Chief". The Charles Dickens Coffee House occupies the ground floor. Dickens maintained a bachelor flat in later years here, even though he had a home to go to. Years later the office boy recalled how Dickens used to send him to fetch ice-cream from a nearby restaurant. After Dickens's death, in 1872, some Chicago businessmen had the idea of purchasing the building and transporting it to the Chicago World Fair, as a memento of the novelist.

On one occasion in 1865 Dickens was eating out at a local coffee-shop in this area and the young Thomas Hardy, then studying architecture in London, spied him. "I went up," the future novelist recalled, "and stood at the vacant place beside the stool on which Dickens was sitting. I had eaten my lunch, but I was quite prepared to eat another if the occasion would make Dickens speak to me. I hoped he would look up, glance at this strange young man beside him and make a remark – if it was only about the weather. But he did nothing of the kind. He was fussing about the bill. So I never spoke to him."

One block to the north-east is the covered Covent Garden. Dickens always loved this area. **We have never outgrown the whole region of Covent Garden**, he wrote in 1853. He recalled that to go there as a child was to inhale **the flavour of the faded cabbage-leaves as if it were the very breath of comic fiction**. He was nostalgic about the place. Covent Garden used to be the wholesale market in London for fruit and vegetables. In January – when there was no seasonable fruit – it was desolate, Dickens wrote in an article that was reprinted in *The Uncommercial Traveller*. A general description of Covent Garden appears in *Little Dorrit*. In *Oliver Twist* Bill Sikes observed that he could find fifty boy thieves at any time at **"Common Garden"**, as he used to call it. And Job Trotter in *Pickwick Papers* spent a night here in a vegetable basket.

At the Tavistock Hotel, north of the covered shopping area, Dickens stayed in late 1844, breaking his residence in Genoa, in order to come to London to read *The Chimes* to his friends. Herbert Pocket and Mr Pip, in *Great Expectations*, used to hold fortnightly meetings of the club, "The Finches of the Grove" at the Hotel. The club's objective was **that the members should dine expensively once a fortnight, quarrel among themselves as much as possible after dinner, and get six waiters drunk on the stairs.**

To the north-west is the area of Seven Dials. Dickens used to walk through this area as a child, sometimes with his father. **What wild visions**, he recalled, **of prodigies of wickedness, want, and beggary arose in my mind out of that place!** He located **the little dark greasy shop** belonging to the taxidermist, Mr Venus, in *Our Mutual Friend*, at Seven Dials. Mr Venus talked about his shop to Silas Wegg: "**My working bench. My young man's bench. A Wice. Tools. Bones, warious. Skulls, warious. Preserved Indian baby. African ditto. Bottled preparations, warious. Everything within reach of your hand, in good preservation… .**"

North of Russell Street is Bow Street and on the right is a

Palladian white stone building that was until 2005 Bow Street Magistrates' Court. There are plans to turn the site into a boutique hotel. The building of 1879 replaces an older Police Court where Barnaby Rudge was interrogated after his participation in the anti-Catholic riots of 1780 known as the Gordon Riots. It is also where the Artful Dodger, in *Oliver Twist*, stated his views of the justice of the procedures: **"This ain't the shop for justice; besides which my attorney is a-breakfasting this morning with the Vice-President of the House of Commons; but I shall have something to say elsevere, and so will he, and so will a wery numerous and respectable circle of acquaintances, as'll make them beaks wish they'd never been born."**

The Opera House is on the site of the Covent Garden Theatre, destroyed by fire in 1856. It is where David Copperfield saw "Julius Caesar" on his first night as a young man in London – he had been staying at the Golden Cross Hotel. **To have all those noble Romans alive before me, and walking in and out for my entertainment, instead of being the stern taskmasters they had been at school, was a most novel and delightful effect.**

Opposite and to the north of the Opera House is Broad Court. Mr Snevellici, the actor in the troupe of Mr Vincent Crummles, said he could be found **in Broad Court, Bow Street, when I'm in town. If I'm not at home, let any man ask for me at the stage-door.**

Facing the north end of Bow Street is the site of St Martin's Hall, where Dickens gave the first of his paid readings in 1858. There was a large and expectant audience when Dickens arrived. He was greeted with a roar which, as an eye-witness observed, "might have been heard at Charing Cross". Some years after that, the Hall was burnt down to be replaced by a theatre. It is now part of a nondescript block of flats and offices.

If we turn right on to Long Acre we meet Drury Lane, just before Freemasons' Hall. This Hall was the venue for a banquet given by

Dickens's friends before his second tour of the United States in 1867. There were 450 guests (all men) but with 100 women in the gallery above. The Union Jack and the Stars and Stripes were entwined and when Dickens appeared on the arm of Bulwer Lytton, "a cry rang through the room, handkerchiefs were waved on the floor and in the galleries ... and the band struck up a full march." There were speeches from Anthony Trollope and Bulwer Lytton. When Dickens rose to reply there was almost pandemonium. Tears streamed down his face as he replied, **Your resounding cheers just now would have been but so many cruel reproaches to me if I could not here declare that, from the earliest days of my career down to this proud night, I have always tried to be true to my calling.**

Turning right into Drury Lane, we pass the back of Drury Lane Theatre and pass the site – overtaken by developments in the 1890s that obliterated the burial ground, attached to the church of St Mary-le-Strand. On the same side there is another small burial site, turned into a minute garden, which used to be part of the parish burial ground of St Martin-in-the-Fields. The Burial Ground, now destroyed and lost, is described in *Bleak House* as **pestiferous and obscene, with houses looking in on every side, save where a reeking little tunnel of a court gives access to the iron gate.** Here Captain Hawdon, otherwise Nemo, was buried. As Joe described the burial to Lady Dedlock, **"Over yinder. Among them piles of bones, and close to that there kitchin winder! ... They put him wery nigh the top. They was obliged to stamp upon it to git it in. I could unkiver it for you with my broom, if the gate was open. That's why they locks it, I s'pose. It's always locked. Look at that rat! Hi! Look! There he goes! Ho! Into the ground."** And here Lady Dedlock was found dead.

A little further towards The Strand there used to be a court on the left – Clare Court. Dickens as a boy, with a few earned pennies in his hand and a loaf of bread under his arm, called here, **magnificently** ordering a small plate of *a la mode* beef to eat with it. What the waiter thought of such a small apparition, coming in all alone, I don't know, but I can see him now, staring at me as I ate my dinner, and bringing up the other waiter to look. I gave him a half-penny, and I wish now that he hadn't taken it.

On the other side of The Strand is Surrey Street. Fifty yards towards the river is an easily missed pedestrian path – Surrey Steps – that takes us to Strand Lane, the access of which to The Strand itself is blocked. At number 6 are the Roman Baths, administered by the National Trust. These are just outside the walls of Roman London. David Copperfield **had many a cold plunge** here. The baths are usually closed but can be opened by special arrangement. Mostly one has to be content with peering through the grubby windows to get an idea of the baths.

The next road to the east leading from The Strand towards the river is Arundel Street, formerly Norfolk Street. The street names of their area indicate that this area of the The Strand was part of the London mansion of the Dukes of Norfolk. Their family name was – and still is – Howard; the Earl of Surrey was a courtesy title given to the Dukes, and Arundel was their Sussex seat. On the left, beyond Maltravers (formerly Howard) Street, was Mrs Lirriper's Lodgings, **Number Eighty-one Norfolk Street Strand – situated midway between the City and St James's and within five minutes' walk of the principal places of public amusement.** Norfolk Street was **a delightful street to lodge in.** Her lodgings were the location of stories in the Christmas numbers of *All the Year Round* in 1863 and 1864 and available in the Penguin edition of *Selected Short Fiction*. Most of the nineteenth-century buildings have been replaced by boring concrete and glass blocks and it is not possible to locate where Mrs Lirriper queened it over her tenants.

Mrs Lirriper had been married in St Clement Danes Church which stands on the island just to the east of Aldwych. She still retained **a very pleasant pew with genteel company and my own hassock and being partial to evening service not too crowded.** The Church is the "parish church" of the Royal Air Force. It contains books of remembrance not only of RAF personnel killed during the Second World War, but also of 16,000 United States personnel who were killed in action while stationed in the United Kingdom. The church was bombed during that war and reconstructed afterwards. The organ over the western gallery was the gift in 1956 of the United States Air Force, their families and friends, to the rebuilt church.

If we go into Aldwych and walk up Kingsway, a street built only at the beginning of the twentieth century, and take the second on the right we go into Sardinia Street. Until 1910 there used to be a Roman Catholic chapel attached to the Italian Embassy. The chapel's history went back to the seventeenth century, when it was attached to the residence of the Sardinian Ambassador. In 1780 it had been a target of the anti-Catholic Gordon rioters and the attack on the chapel is discussed by characters in *Barnaby Rudge*. Dickens's musical sister, Fanny, was a professional singer and met her husband, Henry Burnett, here.

The first road on the right is Portsmouth Street. A few yards on this road on the left is a house, allegedly "The Old Curiosity Shop" in the novel of that name. This is unlikely, for at the end of the novel, the old house is alleged to have been **long ago pulled down.** Moreover this shop only received this name in 1868, twenty years after the publication of the novel. The owner, a dealer in old books, paintings and china, adopted the name to help his business. It is nonetheless an interesting house, a rare survival in this area from the seventeenth century.

The public house further down on the right, The George the Fourth, is more likely to have been the location of the Magpie and Stump, where Mr Lowten, Perker's clerk, in *Pickwick Papers* used to meet up with friends. There is a Magpie and Stump in Fetter Lane nearby, but Dickens placed the pub near Clare Market which is just a few yards away.

To the east runs Portugal Street. (The last stocks used for punishment were set up in this street, in 1820.) In *Pickwick Papers* Tony Weller and fellow coach drivers used to meet in a public house in this road, probably on the southern side.

The gardens to the north are Lincoln's Inn Fields. On the left (western) side, number 58 was the home of Dickens's friend, agent and biographer John Forster. It was here in 1844 that Dickens gave his first reading of *The Chimes* to a group of friends who included the historian Thomas Carlyle, the artist Daniel Maclise and the journalist Douglas Jerrold. The house was also where the lawyer, Mr Tulkinghorn, in *Bleak House* lived … . and died, murdered. **It is a large house, formerly a house of state … It is let off in sets of chambers now: and in those shrunken fragments of its greatness, lawyers lie, like maggots in nuts.**

To the north-west of the Fields is the alleyway, Little Turnstile, that leads on to High Holborn.

Fountain Court Middle Temple

From Lincoln's Inn Fields to the Mansion House

This walk takes us through legal London, three of the four Inns of Court. There are many traces of Bleak House. *We pass by St Paul's Cathedral and end up with some of the sites in the City of London.*

CHANCERY LANE IS the spine of legal London. There are four Inns of Court, long established bodies of lawyers that have the power to acknowledge lawyers who have qualified as Barristers-at-Law. Gray's Inn faces the northern end of Chancery Lane and Inner Temple and Middle Temple face the southern end. The Royal Courts of Justice are just to the west and the Old Bailey less than a mile to the east. When the courts are sitting, the area is full of busy bewigged people bustling around. And has been for centuries. When the courts are not sitting, the area is, said Dickens in *Bleak House*, like **tidal harbours at low water; where stranded proceedings, offices at anchor, idle clerks lounging on top-sided stools ... lie high and dry upon some ooze of the long vacation.**

Lincoln's Inn is off Chancery Lane and at the heart of lawyers' London. It is a collegiate centre that provides accommodation, training and services for barristers. Membership is similar to membership of the colleges of the Universities of Oxford and Cambridge. Lincoln's

Inn can trace its history back to the early fifteenth century. An "Inn" in those days was a term used for the London base of a grandee or bishop, and provided a home for all the potentate's hangers-on. The grandee after whom this Inn is named is either an Earl of Lincoln or a lawyer, Thomas de Lincoln – both individuals of the fourteenth century. Dickens contrasted the apparent rusticity of Lincoln's Inn Fields with the legal process. **In these pleasant fields the sheep are all made into parchment, the goats into wigs, and the pasture into chaff, the lawyer smoke-dried and faded, dwelling among mankind but not consorting with them, aged without experience of genial youth.**

For over a century and a half the main entrance to Lincoln's Inn has been from the eastern side of Lincoln's Inn Fields, from Serle Street, through a brick gatehouse. We pass the extensive New Square, dating back to the late seventeenth century, on the right and have the Old Hall, next to the chapel, ahead of us, overlooking Old Square to the left.

The Old Hall is a small construction of the late fifteenth century, just before Columbus "discovered" America. Over the years the Old Hall has served as a dining hall and a court of justice. It was here that the case of Jarndyce vs Jarndyce in *Bleak House* was held over the years although the final verdict was given in Westminster Hall. **London. Michaelmas Term lately over, and the Lord Chancellor sitting in Lincoln's Inn Hall. Implacable November weather ... Fog everywhere. Fog up the river, where it flows among green aits and meadows; fog down the river, where it rolls defiled among the tiers of shipping, and the waterside pollutions of a great (and dirty) city ... And hard by Temple Bar, in Lincoln's Inn Hall, at the very heart of the fog, sits the Lord High Chancellor in his High Court of Chancery.** Thus the opening chapter of *Bleak House*. When Dickens was writing this the Old Hall was becoming obsolete. Moreover membership of Lincoln's Inn was expanding. So a second central Hall, the Great Hall, was constructed, and opened in 1845, eight years before the publication of *Bleak House*. It was the Court of Chancery that specialised in issues of finance and property. Hence the Jarndyce case which was originally a dispute over inheritance, with **bills, cross-bills, answers, rejoinders, injunctions, affidavits, issues, references to masters, masters' reports – mountains of costly nonsense.** Such a case was not untypical. The inheritance of a huge estate would be referred to the Court of Chancery. When it was resolved who was the legal beneficiary, there was no money left because the whole estate had been devoured by legal fees. **This is the Court of Chancery, which has its decaying and its blighted** lands in every shire and which has its worn-out lunatics in every madhouse and its dead in every churchyard … .Suffer any wrong that can be done you, rather than come here.

Lincoln's Inn chapel is above an undercroft. There are some tombstones among the pavings, and in earlier centuries mothers sometimes abandoned babies here. They were always looked after by the Honourable Society of Lincoln's Inn and usually given the name Lincoln. Access to the chapel is up stone steps. The chapel was built between 1619 and 1623. Inside is a memorial tablet to Spencer Perceval, the only British Prime Minister (so far) to have been assassinated – and that was in May 1812. A chapel bell chimes in the middle of the day when a senior member of the Inn has died. The poet John Donne was Divinity Reader at Lincoln's Inn when he wrote *Devotions*, which contain the lines, "Never send to know for whom the bell tolls; it tolls for thee." He probably had this custom of the Lincoln's Inn chapel bell in mind. The words also provided the inspiration for the title of Ernest Hemingway's novel. Being a Reader of the chapel has often been a useful stepping stone to preferment in the Church of England. Several bishops and one archbishop (Tillotson in the seventeenth century) were formerly Divinity Readers at Lincoln's Inn.

We go past the Dining Hall and the Library on the left and New Square on the right.

In *Bleak House*, Miss Flite, a hopeful beneficiary of the outcome of the case, used to wait on one side of the Hall, day after day, **always expecting some incomprehensible judgment in her favour.** She herself lived **in a narrow back street, part of some courts and lanes immediately outside the wall of the inn.**

In the Old Square Kenge and Carboy had their offices – in the north-west corner, at number 10. Esther Summerson describes her first visit there: **We passed into sudden quietude, under an old gateway, and down on through a silent square, until we came to an old nook in a corner, where there was an entrance up a steep** broad flight of stairs, like an entrance to a church. The steep broad flight of stairs can still be identified.

Mr Pickwick's counsel, Sergeant Snubbin, also had his chambers in this square.

An alleyway, Bishop's Court, goes from New Square by the left of the architecturally inappropriate Hardwicke Building, built in the late 1960s, to Star Lane. To the left was located Krook's Rag and Bottle Warehouse, described in *Bleak House*. The shop was blinded by the wall of Lincoln's Inn intercepting the light within a couple of yards. Above the shop lodged Miss Flite. She lived at the top of the house, in a pretty large room, from which she had a glimpse of the roof of Lincoln's Inn Hall. Above her a room was occupied by Captain Hawdon, alias Nemo. After he died it was taken over by Mr Tony Weevle.

Running off Bishop's Court to the south is Star Yard. At the junction with Chichester Rents there used to be a public house, The Old Ship Tavern, disguised as The Sol's Arms in *Bleak House* and the location for the inquest of Captain Hawdon. It was also a venue for popular singers. The coroner is to sit in the first-floor room at the Sol's Arms, where the Harmonic Meetings take place twice a week, and where the chair is filled by a gentleman of professional celebrity, faced by Little Swills the comic vocalist.

Chancery Lane is where Tom Jarndyce in despair blew his brains out. Off Chancery Lane opposite Lincoln's Inn is Cursitor Street. Immediately on the left was Harold Skimpole's sponging house, Coavinses' Castle.

Off Cursitor Street to the left is Took's Court, a shady place, which was Cook's Court in *Bleak House* and the location of Mr Snagsby's residence and law stationer's shop. The little drawing-room upstairs commanded a view of Cook's Court at one end (not to mention a squint into Cursitor Street) and of Coavinses', the Sheriff's Officer's, backyard on the other. Here Mrs Snagsby entertained her

"Chaplain-in-Ordinary", the Reverend Mr Chadband. Mr Snagsby retreated in his imagination into dreams of a rural past. He would tell his assistants that **a brook once ran down Holborn, when Turnstile really was a turnstile leading slap away into the meadows.**

Bream's Buildings, the road parallel to and to the south of Cursitor Street marked the northern boundary of Symond's Inn, another former inn of court. It was, in Dickens's words, **a little, pale, wall-eyed, woe-begone inn, like a large dust-bin of two compartments and a sifter. It looks as if Symond were a sparing man in his way, and constructed his inn of old building materials, which took kindly to the dry rot and the dirt, and perpetuated Symond's name with congenial shabbiness.** In *Bleak House* the lawyer of Richard Carstone, Mr Vholes, lived here. **Mr Vholes's chambers are on so small a scale, that one clerk can open the door without getting off his stool, while the other who elbows him at the same desk has equal facilities for poking the fire.** Richard lived next door with his new wife, Ada. Esther Summerson used to visit them in this **miserable corner which my dear girl brightened.** But Symond's Inn was also of major importance in Dickens's own life. In 1827, at the age of fifteen, Dickens worked here with a solicitor, Charles Molloy. Here he developed his huge disdain for the profession, which was displayed most powerfully in *Bleak House*. Near Symond's Inn Mr Snagsby used **to lounge about of a Saturday afternoon, and to remark (if in good spirits) that there were old times once.**

If we double back on Chancery Lane, heading south, we can turn right into Carey Street and then first left into Bell Yard; the name of this road forms the title of chapter 15 of *Bleak House*. Here dwelt Gridley, **the man from Shropshire**, and Neckett, the servitor at Coavinses. Bell Yard leads to Fleet Street, to Temple Bar, that used to be the western entrance to the City of London.

On the south side of Fleet Street is Child's Bank, now part of the Royal Bank of Scotland Group. It is the oldest bank in London, dating back to 1664. It has always had close relations with the legal profession, being the bank for the Honourable Societies of Lincoln's Inn and of Middle Temple. The building is a heavy Italian Renaissance revival building and dates back only to 1879. Its predecessor was the model for Tellson's Bank in *The Tale of Two Cities*.

Tellson's Bank, by Temple Bar, was an old-fashioned place even in the year 1780. It was very small, very dark, very ugly, very incommodious. Any one of the partners would have disinherited his son on the question of rebuilding Tellson's. Thus it came to pass that Tellson's was the triumphant perfection of inconvenience. After bursting open a door of idiotic obstinacy with a weak rattle in its throat, you fell into Tellson's, down two steps, and came to your senses in a miserable little shop, with two little counters; where the oldest of men made your cheque shake as if the wind rustled it, while they examined the signature by the dingiest of windows, which were always under a shower-bath of mud from Fleet Street, and which were made the dingier by their own iron bars proper and the shadow of Temple Bar.

Just to the east is Middle Temple Lane. Further east above Inner Temple Lane at 17 Fleet Street is a building that was erected in 1610. Upstairs is Prince Henry's Room, perhaps named after a son of King James I. In the nineteenth century a Mrs Salmon had a display of waxworks here. David Copperfield brought his old nurse, Peggotty, **to see some perspiring waxworks in Fleet Street.** And here at Inner Temple Gate Bradley Headstone in *Our Mutual Friend* jealously stalked Eugene Wrayburn, waiting for him to come out at the gate so he could follow him to see if he was going to see Lizzie Hexam.

Dickens seems to have more positive impressions of the Temple than those stirred by Lincoln's Inn and the Court of Chancery. In 1839 he was at the height of his early success. Nonetheless, perhaps conscious of the bankruptcy of Sir Walter Scott and the vagaries of literary fame, he considered the fallback of a legal career and actually registered as a law student at the Middle Temple. Other members of the Inner Temple have included John Dickinson who drafted the United States Declaration of Independence; five other signatories of the Declaration had been members of the Middle Temple.

The Middle Temple and the Inner Temple are two more of the Inns of Court. In medieval times it was the headquarters of the Templars, those monastic knights whose order was founded in the Holy Land to form a military profession to defend Crusader acquisitions. The Order was dissolved in the fourteenth century and their estates handed over to the Order of Knights Hospitallers who had had a similar history and connection with the Holy Land. Lawyers settled in this area and both the Inner Temple and the Middle Temple, like the other Inns of Court, became a centre for legal training and fellowship. Although each Inn has its own identity and rules of governance, it is not easy for the lay visitor to distinguish one from the other. The Middle Temple is larger and to the west. The Inner Temple is on the eastern side. Between the two is the Temple Church, built around 1185, with the Dome of the Rock on the Temple Mount in Jerusalem as the model. A round chancel is attached to a rectangular nave.

In *Pickwick Papers* Dickens described how, **scattered about in various holes and crevices of the Temple, are certain dark and dirty chambers, in and out of which all the morning in vacation, and half the evening too, in term time, there may be seen constantly hurrying with bundles of papers under their arms and protruding from their pockets an almost uninterrupted succession of lawyers' clerks. There are several grades of lawyers' clerks – there is the articled clerk, who is a lawyer in perspective, who runs a tailor's bill, receives invitations to parties, knows a family in Gower Street, another in Tavistock Square, goes out of town every long vacation to see his father, and is, in short, the very aristocrat of clerks.** (Dickens had already lived in Gower Street and was to have a house in Tavistock Sqaure for ten years.) He came back to the Temple in *Barnaby Rudge*: those who pace its lanes and squares may yet hear the echoes of their footsteps on the sounding stones, and read upon its gates, "Who enter here, leave none behind." There is yet in the Temple something – a clerkly, monkish atmosphere – which public officers of law have not disturbed, and even legal firms have failed to scare away.

If we turn down Middle Temple Lane, beyond Brick Court and off to the right we arrive, a hundred yards towards the river, at Fountain Court. There **was the plash of falling water in fair Fountain Court, and there are yet nooks and corners where dun-haunted students may look down from their dusty garrets, on a vagrant ray of sunlight patching the shade of the tall houses.** It was in Fountain Court that, in *Martin Chuzzlewit*, Ruth Pinch used to meet her brother, Tom, because **it would have been very awkward for her to have had to wait in any but a quiet spot; and that was as quiet a spot, everything considered, as they could choose.** She would also meet her future husband, John Westlock, by the fountain. When he turned up **merrily the fountain leaped and danced, and merrily the smiling dimples twinkled and expanded more and more.** It is still a favourite place for luncheon rendezvous. A plaque by the fountain records: **Brilliantly the Temple Fountain sparkled in the sun, and laughingly, its liquid music played and merrily the idle drops of water danced and danced, and peeping out in sport among the trees, plunged lightly down to hide themselves.** The mood is very different from the fog and despair of Lincoln's Inn. The present fountain was (re)constructed in 1975.

At the end of Fountain Court was Garden Court to the left and heading down towards the river. Here, in *Great Expectations*, was the shared chambers of Mr Pip and Herbert Pocket. **We lived at the top of the house.** And here, Pip's benefactor, Magwitch, turned up unexpectedly, and Pip had to find a temporary home for him **at a lodging-house in Essex-street, the back of which looked into the**

Temple, and was almost within hail of Pip's window. Essex Street is another street leading from Fleet Street to the river, immediately to the west of Garden Court.

There was once a jetty on the river, Temple Stairs, long since swept away by the building of the Embankment. But today there is an archway, built in 1868, with boys riding dolphins in bronze, and a tablet recording the name of this stretch of water The King's Reach, in commemoration of the Silver Jubilee of King George V in 1935. Mr Pip, in *Great Expectations*, kept a boat here and practised rowing up and down the river. From here he smuggled his patron, Magwitch, down the river to a steamer near Gravesend. In preparing for this section of the novel Dickens made a note of tides and their times, and hired a Thames steamer to get the feel of a pursuit down the river.

Returning to Middle Temple Lane and going through a passage to the east opposite Brick Court, we can enter Pump Court where Tom Pinch may well have been installed as librarian. Dickens describes the neighbourhood as Mr Fips, the agent for an unknown patron, escorted Tom **through sundry lanes and courts, into one more quiet and gloomy than the rest; and singling out a certain house, ascended a common stairway.**

The grave of Oliver Goldsmith, one of Dickens's favourite writers, is outside the Temple Church. The present Goldsmith's Buildings have replaced the buildings where Mortimer Lightwood and Eugene Wrayburn in *Our Mutual Friend* had chambers.

Further to the east, we go past the southern wall of the Temple Church and through another archway to King's Bench Walk. On the eastern side is Tudor gate, which, as Whitefriars Gate, was where Mr Pip in *Great Expectations* received the message from Wemmick: **"Don't go home."** Facing the Walk is Paper Buildings, on the west side. The present buildings date from the 1830s and 1840s, replacing buildings where the odious Sir Edward Chester, in *Barnaby Rudge*, had chambers. Nearby were also the chambers of Mr Stryver, who was served by Sydney Carton in *A Tale of Two Cities.*

In 1869 Dickens was delighted to show his American friends, James T and Annie Adam Fields, round the Temple area. He showed them the sites associated with the events of *Great Expectations*, almost as if there was no difference between fact and his fiction.

If we return to Fleet Street, just to the east of Chancery Lane on the north is Clifford's Inn Passage, where Mr Rokesmith, in *Our Mutual Friend*, withdrew from the bustle of Fleet Street with Mr Boffin, to offer his services as secretary. Mr Boffin **glanced into the mouldy little plantation, or cat preserve, of Clifford's Inn as it was that day ... Sparrows were there, dry-rot and wet-rot were there; but it was not otherwise a suggestive place.**

St Dunstan's-in-the-West Church used to have a fountain where Hugh, in *Barnaby Rudge*, drenched himself in order to sober up, before calling on Sir John Chester at Paper Buildings. The fountain by the entrance, however, dates only from 1860. The church clock dates from 1671. The chiming of the church clock woke Scrooge in *A Christmas Carol.* David Copperfield came here with Betsey Trotwood to watch the giants strike the bells at noon one day. And Dickens dedicated his Christmas story, *The Chimes*, to this church.

Fleet Street used to be the centre of the British newspaper industry. There are a few traces of that activity – a bust of Lord Northcliffe, the founder of *The Daily Mail* in 1894, the first modern popular newspaper

If we continue east along Fleet Street, we come to Johnson's Court on the left. The *Monthly Magazine* had its offices here. They published Dickens's first story – "A Dinner in Poplar Walk" – in 1833. The address was number 166 Fleet Street, but the letter-box, through which Dickens posted his story, was in the archway that gives access to the Court; **it was dropped stealthily one evening at twilight, with fear and trembling, into a dark letter-box in a dark office up** a dark court in Fleet Street. White concrete buildings have replaced newspaper offices. We pass, on the right, Bouverie Street, where Dickens's publishers, Bradbury and Evans, had their offices.

The next street on the right is Whitefriars Street. At the junction of that street and Fleet Street was the home of *The Daily News,* of which Charles Dickens was editor for a few days in 1846. Brief though his time as editor was, he managed nonetheless to employ his father as manager of the parliamentary reporting staff and his father-in-law as music and dramatic critic. The building was demolished at the end of the nineteenth century. Some instalments of *Pictures from Italy* were published in the newspaper. *The Daily News* was a Liberal paper that merged with another Liberal paper, *The Daily Chronicle*, in 1930 to form the *News Chronicle*, which, in turn, folded up in 1960. Jerry Cruncher, in *A Tale of Two Cities*, had rooms in Hanging Sword Alley, to the left off Whitefriars Street at the Fleet Street end. **They were not in a savoury neighbourhood, and were but two in number, even if a closet with a single pane of glass in it may be counted as one.** No buildings from the nineteenth century have survived. Indeed most of the corporate buildings date from after the Second World War.

Back on Fleet Street, if we cross the road to the northern side and turn left into Wine Office Court, we find Ye Olde Cheshire Cheese on the right, rebuilt in 1667 after the Fire of London. Here Charles Darnay, in *The Tale of Two Cities*, having been acquitted of high treason, dined with Sidney Carton. They had left the Old Bailey and, arm in arm, went **down Ludgate Hill to Fleet Street, and so up a covered way into a tavern.** The public house has other classic literary associations. It was a favourite of Dr Samuel Johnson and of Oliver Goldsmith, as well as Thackeray and Dickens himself. Dickens is reckoned to have had his favourite seat here – at a table to the right of the fireplace on the ground floor in what is today called the Chop Room to the left of the entrance.

On the floor of the Wine Office Court is a plaque in a paving stone with the totally incorrect suggestion that this marked the site of Mrs Lirriper's Lodgings, in the story published in *All the Year Round* in 1863. They were in fact half a mile to the south-west in Arundel Street.

On to Ludgate Circus. To the left is Farringdon Street, which follows the course of the now submerged River Fleet. If we go up Farringdon Street as far as the bridge over the road, Holborn Viaduct, we reach the site of Fleet Market, described in *Barnaby Rudge* as **a long irregular row of wooden sheds and pent-houses occupying the centre of what is now called Farringdon Street.** Until the 1950s there survived a second-hand book market on stalls in Farringdon Street, the last survival of the market.

On the east side of Farringdon Street, nearer Ludgate Circus, just to the south of Old Fleet Lane is the site of the Fleet Prison, where Mr Pickwick, attended by Sam Weller, was incarcerated until the costs of the shady lawyers, Dodson and Fogg, had been settled. The prison went back to the Middle Ages and used to occupy an island among the creeks and canals of the Fleet River that rose on Hampstead Heath and flowed into the Thames. It has long since been driven underground, but it is possible, in places, to follow its course. The River Fleet became a noisome sewer. The prison was burnt down during the Gordon Riots, as narrated in *Barnaby Rudge*, and rebuilt in the 1780s. Dickens described the prison when Mr Pickwick was there, with **a long narrow gallery, dirty and low, paved with stone, and very dimly lighted by a window at each remote end.** The prison was closed in 1842 and the building pulled down in 1844. It has been replaced on the southern side by a succession of buildings, the latest being another plate glass and concrete construction, put up at the beginning of the twenty-first century and already heading for stylistic obsolescence. It replaced a building of 1972, which itself replaced a building, the Congregational Memorial

Hall, of 1872 that was built after the demolition of the Fleet Prison. In this hall the British Labour Party was founded in February 1900.

Between Ludgate Circus and St Paul's Cathedral, shortly on the left is where the Belle Sauvage Inn stood until the 1830s. It was an old coaching inn. Originally called The Bell, it had a landlord called Mr Savage: whence the name. Sam Weller told the story of his father's interrogation at the time of his father's marriage.

"'What is your name, sir?' says the lawyer. 'Tony Weller,' says my father. 'Parish?' says the lawyer. 'Belle Savage,' says my father; for he stopped there when he drove up, and he know'd nothing about parishes, *he* didn't."

There is no trace of this inn, not even a name. Nor is there any sign of the London Coffee House, where the All Bar One coffee bar is. Arthur Clennam, in *Little Dorrit*, first stayed here when he arrived in London from overseas. He sat contemplatively looking out of the window, **in the same place as the day died, looking at the dull houses opposite, and thinking, if the disembodied spirits of former inhabitants were ever conscious of them, how they must pity themselves for their old places of imprisonment ... Presently the rain began to fall in slanting lines between him and those houses, and people began to collect under cover of the public passage opposite, and to look hopelessly at the sky as the rain dropped thicker and thicker.** The coffee house, which was founded in 1731, was a favourite resort of Americans. Benjamin Franklin was a member of a club that met to discuss philosophical issues here, and George Peabody, the philanthropist from Baltimore, in 1851 hosted a dinner for Americans connected with the Great Exhibition of that year.

Then St Paul's Cathedral, which so impressed the Yorkshireman, John Browdie, in *Nicholas Nickleby*: **"See there, lass, there be Paul's Church. Ecod, he be a soizable one, he be."** In 1856, at London's celebration of the conclusion of the Crimean War, Dickens obtained special permission to go to the gallery on the outside of the dome to watch the illuminations and display of fireworks. It was by the clock of the cathedral that Ralph Nickleby adjusted his own watch. Mr Pip, in *Great Expectations*, used the **great black dome** of the cathedral to work out where he was in the city. Jo, the crossing-sweeper in *Bleak House*, is puzzled by the cross on the top of the dome. And Peggotty in *David Copperfield*, brought here by David, is disappointed because it is not like the picture she has of it on her work-box.

To the right of the cathedral is Dean's Court, leading to Carter Lane Youth Hostel. Further south towards the river was Doctors' Commons where Dickens worked for a while in his early twenties. In *David Copperfield* he described it as **a little out-of-the-way place where they administer what is called ecclesiastical law, and play all kinds of tricks with obsolete monsters of Acts of Parliament, which three-fourths of the world know nothing about.** A plaque on the Faraday Building in Queen Victoria Street commemorates Doctors Commons, which Mr Boffin in *Our Mutual Friend* personalised as **Doctor Scommons.** The offices of the lawyers, Spenlow and Jorkins, in *David Copperfield*, were in the vicinity. On the south side of Carter Lane to the east of Dean's Court there used to be a public house, the Bell Tavern, frequented by Dickens as he prepared *David Copperfield.* The New Bell Yard is the sole reminder of this association.

In the crypt of St Paul's Cathedral lies the body of George Cruikshank (1792–1878), the illustrator of *Sketches by Boz* and *Oliver Twist*.

The area to the north of St Paul's Cathedral used to be full of booksellers and small publishers. There is a story that Dickens was walking there and gazed at a picture of himself in a bookshop window. A boy by him was looking at the same image and then looked up at Dickens with awesome surprise. Dickens laughed and gave a nod acknowledging his identity before walking off briskly along Cheapside. For much of his life he became a distinctively public figure. His son, Henry, wrote that "to walk with him in the streets of London was a revelation ... people of all degrees and classes taking off their hats and greeting him as he passed."

Cheapside is to the north-east of the Cathedral and leads to the financial heart of the city. When Dickens was eleven and before he worked at the blacking factory, he lost himself in the Strand and wandered into the City, **like a child in a dream, staring at the British merchants, and inspired by a mighty faith in the marvellousness of everything. Up courts and down courts – in and out of yards and little squares – peeping into counting house passages and running away.**

The third street on the left is Wood Street, which used to have the inn, The Cross Keys. This was one of twenty-five coaching inns in the City. By the end of the nineteenth century all but one had disappeared, such was the impact of railway transport. It was where Mr Pip arrived in London in *Great Expectations* on his first visit to London. In the same novel, he anxiously awaited the arrival of Estelle. But Dickens himself arrived here at the age of ten, an "unaccompanied minor", on the coach from Chatham. His parents had already settled in London, in Camden Town, and the young Dickens stayed on at a school. **Through all the years that have since passed have I never lost the smell of the damp straw in which I was packed – like game – and forwarded, carriage paid, to the Cross Keys, Wood Street, Cheapside, London.** (David Copperfield, on his arrival in London from Suffolk, was, **by invitation of the clerk on duty, passed behind the counter, and sat down on the scale at which they weighed the luggage.** Mr Mell met him and took him to Salem House, Blackheath. The clerk **slanted me off the scale, and pushed me over to him, as if I were weighed, bought, delivered, and paid for.** But this was at the Blue Boar, Whitechapel.)

The "cross keys" is a symbol of St Peter, who held the keys of

Heaven. Before the Fire of London in 1666 St Peter's Church stood nearby. It was destroyed in the Fire of London and never replaced. The inn was demolished in the 1860s. But a small court on the left has a few gravestones and is all that is left of the connection with St Peter's Church.

St Mary-le-Bow church is on the right hand side of the road. The firm, Dombey and Son, had its principal offices within earshot of the bells of this church.

King Street on the left leads to The Guildhall, or **Gold, or Golden Hall**, as the child Dickens heard it said. The building represents the headquarters of the City of London and was built in the fifteenth century and survived the Fire of London in 1666 and the Blitz of the Second World War. In the City Court here, Mr Pickwick was the defendant in the trial of Bardell vs Pickwick. The Court of Common Pleas from 1822 to 1883 was located in the Gallery, the building to the south-east of the Guildhall itself.

Cheapside morphs into Poultry. Along Grocers' Hall Court to the left there used to be a restaurant in the last building on the right. Here, Sam Weller brought Mr Pickwick for a quiet brandy and water. Here also Mr Pickwick met Sam Weller's father, Tony. There are no restaurants or even separate buildings here today. All is one white impersonal building, part of the Midland Bank complex.

At the end of Poultry on the right is the Mansion House, the residence of the Lord Mayor of London, who, in *The Christmas Carol*, **in the stronghold of the mighty Mansion House, gave orders to his fifty cooks and butlers to keep Christmas as a Lord Mayor's household should.**

And when Mark Tapley, serving Martin Chuzzlewit in the United States, spoke to members of the Watertoast Association about Queen Victoria, he said she **has lodgings, in virtue of her office, with the Lord Mayor at the Mansion House, but don't often occupy them, in consequence of the parlour chimney smoking.**

Raymond's Buildings, Gray's Inn

From Holborn Circus to Soho Square

This walk, which includes an optional two-stop journey on the Underground, takes us to the three major London houses that Dickens lived in. We follow in the steps of Barnaby Rudge *and* Martin Chuzzlewit *and the grim smart streets of the West End, unloved by Dickens.*

WALKING WEST FROM HOLBORN CIRCUS, we pass Fetter Lane on the left and then a branch of the HSBC Bank. This is on the site of Langdale's Distillery which was trashed during the anti-Catholic Gordon Riots in 1780. The proprietor was a Roman Catholic. Dickens describes the scene in *Barnaby Rudge*. At this place a large detachment of soldiery were posted, who fired, now up Fleet Market, now up Holborn, now up Snow Hill – constantly raking the streets in each direction … . Full twenty times, the rioters, headed by one man who wielded an axe in his right hand, and bestrode a brewer's horse of great size and strength, caparisoned with fetters taken out of Newgate, which clanked and jingled as he went, made an attempt to force a passage at this point, and fire the vintner's house … . The vintner's house, with half-a-dozen others near at hand, was one great, glowing

blaze ... . The gutters of the street, and every crack and fissure in the stones, ran with scorching spirit, which being dammed up by busy hands, overflowed the road and pavement, and formed a great pool, into which the people dropped down dead by dozens. They lay in heaps all round this fearful pond, husbands and wives, fathers and sons, mothers and daughters, women with children in their arms and babies at their breasts, and drank until they died.

Mr Langdale and another Catholic, Mr Harewood, were rescued

from the house by a back doorway that led on to the **narrow lane in the rear** [which was] **quite free of people. So, when they had crawled through the passage indicated by the vintner (which was a mere shelving-trap for the admission of casks), and had managed with some difficulty to unchain and raise the door at the upper end, they emerged into the street without being observed or interrupted.** This let them on to Fetter Lane – at a building now replaced by the southern end of the branch of the HSBC Bank.

Next door on the south side is Barnard's Inn, another former lawyers' Inn. Today it consists of a hotchpotch of mostly eighteenth- and nineteenth-century buildings with a series of courtyards, grouped around a sixteenth-century hall. Barnard's Inn used to provide residential accommodation for law students, but today fulfils a variety of functions, commercial and educational. It was occupied until 1959 by Mercers' School attached to the Mercers' Company who own the building. The Company restored it sympathetically in the 1930s and again the 1990s. It serves as the home of the independent Gresham's College. Its attractive refurbishments contrast with the state of the place in Dickens's time. He made Mr Pip in *Great Expectations* describe Barnard's Inn as the **dingiest collection of shabby buildings ever squeezed together in a rank corner as a club for tom-cats.** Pip stayed here with Herbert Pocket for a short while on his first trip to London. Pip was not initially impressed.

We entered this haven through a wicket-gate, and were disgorged by an introductory passage into a melancholy little square that looked to me like a flat burying ground. I thought it had the most dismal trees in it, and the most dismal sparrows, and the most dismal cats, and the most dismal houses (in number half-a-dozen or so), that I had ever seen.

The confident brick Gothic building on the north side of the road, the headquarters of Prudential Assurance, were designed by Waterhouse in the last part of the nineteenth century and are on the site of Furnival's Inn, a block of flats for the then upwardly mobile. Furnival's Inn was another residential block for lawyers studying at Lincoln's Inn. It severed its connection with law in 1817 and Charles Dickens, escaping from his feckless parents, took an apartment here with his brother, Frederick, from 1834 to 1837. The rent was £35 a year. In *Martin Chuzzlewit* he described the Inn as **a shady, quiet place, echoing to the footsteps of the stragglers who have business there, and rather monotonous and gloomy on Sunday evenings**. In the first courtyard up on the right a plaque celebrates Dickens's time here and where he wrote *Sketches by Boz* and much of *Pickwick Papers*.

In 1836 W M Thackeray, seven months older than Dickens, called here on the young successful author. Thackeray knew that Dickens wanted an artist to illustrate his writings, and brought along a portfolio of work. But Dickens did not find them suitable.

After his marriage in 1836, Dickens stayed on in Furnival's Inn, though in another larger apartment. Here his eldest son was born. At the back of the Inn, accessible to it through a square, was Wood's Hotel, where Mr Grewgious in *The Mystery of Edwin Drood* used to go for dinner **three hundred days in the year at least**. He found rooms for Rosa Budd, when she fled from Cloisterham (Rochester). She was provided with a chambermaid and a bedroom and a sitting-room. It was safe, for, as Mr Grewgious said, reassuring her, **"Furnival's is fire-proof, and specially watched and lighted, and *I* live over the way."** Today Furnival's Inn houses the headquarters of English Heritage, as well as banks and the offices of hi-tech companies.

Further west, on the south side of the street is Staple Inn, with a half-timbered facade facing the street. **Behind the most ancient part of Holborn, London, where certain gabled houses some** centuries of age still stand looking at the public way … is a little nook called Staple Inn. It presents the sensation of having put cotton in his [the visitor's] ears and velvet soles on his feet. These half-timbers, the most impressive surviving timber building in London, go back to the sixteenth century. For over a century the half-timbers were plastered over but in 1884 the Inn was acquired by the Prudential Assurance Company who stripped the plaster and restored the timbers. There was more heavy restoration, even reconstruction, in the twentieth century. The Tudor exterior is in sharp contrast to the elegant eighteenth-century inner buildings around a quadrangle. Mr Grewgious, in *The Mystery of Edwin Drood*, had chambers here – at number 10 – as did Neville Landless in the same novel. The chambers overlooked a little garden at the back, where a few smoky sparrows twitter in the smoky trees, as though they had called to each other, "let us play at country". Another resident of Staple Inn was Mr Tartar, also in *The Mystery of Edwin Drood*, who occupied the neatest, the cleanest, and the best-ordered chambers ever seen under the sun, moon, and stars. And Mr Snagsby, the law stationer in *Bleak House*, being in his way rather a meditative and poetical man used to wander around here to observe how countrified the sparrows and the leaves are. Nathaniel Hawthorne came here in 1852. "It was strange to have drifted into it so suddenly out of the bustle and rumble of Holborn." The same is true 160 years later.

Another Inn, that provided a base for lawyers, is Gray's Inn, a few yards along Gray's Inn Road that leads north from High Holborn. It is still one of the four surviving Inns of Court. The Inn is on the left, and can trace its history back to the fourteenth century. It is like the other Inns of Court, with common architectural features, and with family resemblances to colleges at Oxford and Cambridge. Residential and communal buildings are grouped around courts (or squares). In contrast to the rest of London the visitor enjoys a sense of spaciousness. (Be warned, however, that the Inns may be closed to visitors at weekends.) All of Gray's Inn suffered severe war damage in the Second World War and many of the present buildings date from after 1945. There are two squares and extensive gardens.

Charles Dickens was employed as a clerk to Edward Blackmore, an Attorney, between May 1827 – he was just fifteen – to November 1828; his wage ranged between 13s 6d and 15s (67p to 75p) a week. The office where he worked was at number 1, Holborn Court. The Court was renamed South Square in 1829. His office was at the back, overlooking a space between the Inn and the back of Holborn shops, on to which he used to drop cherry-stones. This passage, **a squalid little trench, with rank grass and a pump in it, lying between the coffee-house and South-square**, is now a smart access street for service vehicles and called The Paddock. In the 1820s, it was a grassy area given over to cats and rats.

Tommy Traddles, David Copperfield's chum, had chambers here – at number 2 South Square. He used to ascend by a rickety staircase, **feebly lighted on each landing by a club-headed little oil wick dying away in a little dungeon of dirty glass**. The ever cheer-ful Traddles claimed it was **"a very nice little room when you're up here"**. Mr Perker, Mr Pickwick's legal adviser, also had chambers in Gray's Inn. We do not know exactly where his rooms were beyond the fact that you reached them **after climbing two pairs of steep and dirty stairs**. In *Little Dorrit* Flora Finching, with whom Arthur Clennam had been in love two decades earlier, meets up with Arthur in the gardens of Gray's Inn. For Arthur the reunion is a disaster. When he was writing *Little Dorrit* Dickens had recently met up with his old flame of twenty years earlier, Maria Beadnell, with equal dis-illusion. The account of the reunion in the novel shows Dickens at his cruellest. Maria always read the novels of her old lover and would have been mortified to have seen herself portrayed so savagely.

The legal partnership of Ellis and Blackmore, solicitors, moved – taking Dickens – to number 1, and later number 6, Raymond Buildings. These Buildings can be found to the north-west of the Inn on the road leading to Theobalds Road. They were newly built when Dickens worked there. Flora Finching, in *Little Dorrit*, reminds Arthur Clennam of their old romance when they walked in the gardens at the back of Raymond's Buildings **at exactly four o' clock in the afternoon.**

He derived his early impressions of the legal system and the legal profession during these years, and saw Gray's Inn in 1860, as **that stronghold of Melancholy ... one of the most depressing institutions in brick and mortar, known to the children of men. Can anything be more dreary than its arid Square, Sahara Desert of the law, with the ugly old tiled-topped tenements, the dirty windows, the bills To Let, To Let, the door-posts inscribed like gravestones, the crazy gateway giving upon the filthy Lane, the scowling iron-barred prison-like passage into Verulam-buildings, the mouldy red-nosed ticket-porters with little coffin plates ... the dry hard atomy-like appearance of the whole dust-heap.** Dirt and filth. These were strong words for a man like Dickens who was clean in his habits, and almost dandyish in his dress.

If we leave Gray's Inn by the Holborn Gate that leads on to High Holborn and head west, we pass on the right much twentieth-century development. One street has been lost – Kingsgate Street where in *Martin Chuzzlewit* Poll Sweedlepipe, barber and bird-fancier, had his premises, **next door but one to the celebrated mutton-pie shop, and directly opposite the cat's meat warehouse.** On the first floor dwelt Mrs Gamp, who was often summoned to her duties as night nurse, layer-out of the dead and midwife **by pebbles, walking-sticks, and fragments of tobacco-pipes, all much more efficacious than the street-door knocker, which was so constructed to wake the street with ease, and even spread alarms of fire in**

Holborn, without making the smallest impression on the premises to which it was addressed.

New Oxford Street, which runs 150 yards to the west of Holborn underground station, was built in 1847 to by-pass St Giles High Street. In later years some appalling slum dwellings were destroyed with little consideration given to rehousing the 5,000 people who lived there. (**... never heeding, never asking, where the wretches whom we clear out, crowd**). The whole area of St Giles was notorious for its "rookeries", huge blocks of buildings that were let and sublet. One man would rent a flat, then let each room to a family or families. (St Giles is, appropriately, the patron saint of outcasts.) Dickens used to wander around here, having what his friend and biographer, John Forster, called "a profound attraction of repulsion to St Giles's". In the 1840s famine forced many Irish to migrate to mainland Britain and the United States. Certain parts of London became the homes of exploited Irish families. St Giles was one such and became known as "Little Ireland". In 1850 Dickens toured the area in the company of his police detective friend, Inspector Field, on whom Inspector Bucket in *Bleak House* is based. Tenants settled in **this compound of sickening smells, these heaps of filth, these tumbling houses, with all their vile contents, animate and inanimate, slimily overflowing into the black road ... . Men, women, children, for the most part naked, heaped upon the floor like maggots in a cheese! Ho! In that dark corner yonder! Does anybody lie there? Me sir, Irish me, a widder with six children. And yonder? Me sir, Irish me, with me wife and eight poor babes. And to the left there? Me sir, Irish me, along with two more Irish boys as is me friends. And to the right there? Me sir and the Murphy fam'ly, numbering five blessed souls. And what's this, coiling, now, about my foot? Another Irish me, pitifully in want of shaving, whom I have awakened from sleep – and across my other foot lies his wife – and by the shoes of Inspector**

Field lie their three eldest – and their three youngest are at present squeezed between the open door and the wall. And why is there no one on that little mat before the sullen fire? Because O'Donovan, with his wife and daughter, is not come in from selling Lucifers!

Doubling back we have Southampton Place to the north. This used to be called Southampton Street. It was here – at number 18 – where Mr Grewgious in *The Mystery of Edwin Drood*, found accommodation for Rosa Budd and Miss Twinkleton at the house (or 'ouse) of querulous Mrs Billickin who refused to sign documents using her Christian name for reasons of prudence and security. Two doors away is an archway. "The arching," Mrs Billickin observed, "leads to a mews; mewses must exist."

Southampton Place leads to Bloomsbury Square. To the west of the square is the British Museum. Both Charles Dickens and Mr Pickwick were readers at the library at the British Museum. The former Reading Room was redesigned as the Great Court in the 1990s by Norman Foster. The books, documents and manuscripts were moved to the new British Library by St Pancras Station.

At 29 Bloomsbury Square, on the east side, lived Lord Mansfield, the great eighteenth-century liberal-minded lawyer. His house was destroyed in the Gordon Riots, as described in *Barnaby Rudge*. The trashing of his residence here – he had a country home at Ken (or Caen) Wood, Highgate – led to a **common ruin of the whole of the costly furniture, the plate and jewels, a beautiful gallery of pictures, the rarest collection of manuscripts ever possessed by any one private person in the world, and, worst of all, because nothing could replace the loss, the great Law Library, on almost every page of which were notes, in the judge's own hand, of inestimable value; being the results of the study and experience of his whole life.** (Dickens's hostility to the legal profession seems to have been suspended in the case of Lord

Mansfield.) In the Square two of the rioters were hanged, facing Lord Mansfield's looted residence. The gardens of the square were originally designed by the landscape gardener Humphry Repton in the first years of the nineteenth century. There is no trace of Mansfield's home, the site of which is now occupied by Victoria House, built in 1928 as the then headquarters of the Liverpool and Victoria Friendly Society.

Leaving Bloomsbury Square at the north eastern corner we come after a few yards to Southampton Row. Turning left and then through the passageway, Cosmo Place, on the right, we come to Queen Square. Richard Carstone, in *Bleak House*, had an apartment in this area. It is believed to have been 28 Old Gloucester Street, which exits the square from the south-west angle.

If we head from the south-east along Great Ormond Street we arrive, on the left, at the Great Ormond Street Hospital for Children, founded as a small pediatric hospital in 1852. Charles Dickens presided over a dinner in 1858 held to raise funds for developing its work. He arranged for the proceeds of a public reading of *A Christmas Carol* to be dedicated to the Hospital. In *Our Mutual Friend*, the sick child, Johnny, made his will. **From bed to bed, a light womanly tread and a pleasant fresh face passed in the silence of the night. A little head would lift itself into the softened light here and there, to be kissed as the face went by – for these little patients are very loving – and would then submit itself to be composed to rest again.**

If we turn left, beyond the hospital, into Lamb's Conduit Street we come to face Coram's Fields, on the northern side of Guilford Street. This is on the site of an eighteenth-century charitable refuge for foundling children – the Foundling Hospital. For a while, when Dickens lived at Doughty Street nearby, he regularly attended the Hospital chapel. The servant of the Meagleses in *Little Dorrit*, Harriet Beadle, is called Tattycoram. The first part of the name is a corruption of Harriet, the second in deference to the founder of the Hospital from where she was recruited.

In the eighteenth century this area was the northern limit of built-up London. In *Barnaby Rudge* Sim Tappertit and his friends met at the Boot Tavern: **a lone place of public entertainment, situated in the fields at the back of the Foundling Hospital; a very solitary spot at that period, and quite deserted after dark. The Tavern stood at some distance from any high road, and was only approachable by a dark and narrow lane.** In Cromer Street, just off Judd Street, a quarter of a mile to the north of the Foundling Museum, the Boot public house still exists, the successor of the one Dickens knew. It is by Speedy Place, an alley to the west, filled with potted plants and providing a delightful and unexpected touch of greenery to an otherwise drab neighbourhood. Some of the turrets of St Pancras railway station can be seen to the north. The Speedy family, after whom the alley is named, were for several generations the licensees of the Boot Inn.

Walking east along Guilford Street we reach Doughty Street on the right. After a few houses on the left we come to no 48, now the Dickens Museum. Charles Dickens lived here for less than three years, from 1837, when he was aged twenty-five and newly married, to late 1839. He had moved out of Furnival's Inn and moving here was a confident acknowledgement that he had arrived. The rent was £80 a year and Mr and Mrs Dickens employed three servants. In the 1830s Doughty Street was a private road, gated at each end. There were twelve rooms over four floors. The study where Dickens wrote the last parts of *Pickwick Papers*, *Oliver Twist* and *Nicholas Nickleby* was at the back of the first floor. Mrs Dickens's sister, Mary Hogarth, was living with them. She died suddenly at the house at the age of seventeen. The three of them had gone to the theatre, Mary went up to bed and was heard uttering a choking cry. She died the following afternoon in Dickens's arms. He was so affected that he was unable to complete his allotted serial parts of *Pickwick Papers* and *Oliver Twist* – he was writing both simultaneously. It was a death that scarred Dickens for the rest of his life, and many of his virginal heroines seem to be based on Mary. However within three years Dickens and his family moved out. His wife was usually pregnant and he is reported to have said unsympathetically that **the house in Doughty Street was nothing but a hospital ward**. After Dickens's time the house was divided into flats and served as a boarding house. It was purchased by the Dickens Fellowship in the 1920s and has been a museum ever since.

Let us double back along Guilford Street to Russell Square. Turning right along Woburn Place we come after one block to Tavistock Square. This square was designed in 1824. On the northeast side is the headquarters of the British Medical Association. It occupies the site of Tavistock House that Dickens purchased on a forty-five year lease and which became his London home from 1851 to 1860. It was **decidedly cheap – most commodious – and might be made very handsome**. It was certainly commodious, with eighteen rooms including a drawing-room that could hold over 300 people. There was also a garden, large even then for central London. The kitchen was underground and the bedrooms at the top of the house. Hans Christian Andersen stayed here in 1857. He had "a snug room looking out on the garden, and over the tree-tops I saw the London towers and spires appear and disappear as the weather cleared or thickened." The original building was pulled down in 1901 and today a blue plaque marks the site of his residence here.

The house witnessed highs and lows in Dickens's life. It was where Dickens hosted parties with generous exuberance. Here he would entertain his friends and regiment his family in the performance of amateur dramatics at what became known as the Theatre Royal, Tavistock House. Here he wrote *Bleak House*, *Hard Times* and *Little*

Dorrit. His study was next to a drawing room and was separated from it by sliding doors. When he was thinking hard, he used to open up these doors and stride up and down the length of the two rooms. Tavistock House was also the scene of the progressive disintegration of his marriage. In 1856 his wife's family stayed at the house; Dickens stayed away. Their bohemian untidiness distressed him. When they moved out he returned and at once threw himself into manically spring-cleaning the place. He **opened the windows, aired the carpets, and purified every room from the roof to the hall**. On another occasion he had a row with his wife, got up at two in the morning and walked to his newly-acquired house at Gad's Hill Place near Rochester – thirty miles, arriving there at nine in the morning.

After Dickens gave up his tenancy a later resident was the French composer, Charles Gounod (1818–93). For a while it was also a Jewish College before being demolished in 1900.

Twenty yards to the south of the plaque, on the railings, is another plaque, often accompanied by flowers, marking the site where people were killed following the terrorist outrage of 7 July 2005, ("7/7"). A bomb detonated on a number 30 double-decker bus, killing thirteen people and wounding many others. The names are recorded on the plaque – Muslim, Jewish, Indian, English – reflecting the diversity that is London.

If we leave the square at the south-west angle, pass Gordon Square and negotiate a dog-leg bend we reach Gower Street. On the western side of the street to the north is the site of number 145, just beyond Grafton Way. The former house has been replaced by a vast glass plated building, part of the Elizabeth Garrett Anderson wing of University College Hospital. Charles Dickens's mother lived at number 145 and made a valiant though pathetic attempt to set up a school for young ladies while her husband was in the Marshalsea Prison. Charles lived here briefly – he was ten years old at the time.

The endeavour was a total failure. As Dickens himself recalled, **I left at a great many other doors a great many circulars, calling attention to the merits of the establishment. Yet nobody ever came to school, nor do I recollect that anybody ever proposed to come, or that the least preparation was made to receive anybody. But, I know that we got on very badly with the butcher and baker.** The row of houses was demolished in 1895. Next door there had been a dancing "academy", which may have served as a model for that of Mr Turveydrop in *Bleak House*.

A journey of two stops to the west on the underground from Euston Square station close by brings us to Baker Street. (The underground railway goes under Euston Road, off which to the south is Cleveland Street. In 1814 it was known as Norfolk Street and Dickens and his family lived there briefly between residences in Portsmouth and Chatham. In 1831 Dickens also had lodgings in the same street for a short time. It is the address he gave in his application to consult books at the British Museum.)

To the east and on the south side of Marylebone Road, opposite the Royal Academy of Music, is St Marylebone parish church. It was probably in the church that Paul Dombey was christened, and later buried alongside his mother, and where his father married Edith Grainger. **The tall shrouded pulpit and reading desk; the dreary perspective of empty pews stretching away under the galleries and empty benches mounting to the roof and lost in the shadow of the great grim organ; the dusty matting and the cold stone slabs; the grisly free-seats in the aisles; and the damp corner by the bell-rope, where the black tressels used for funerals were stowed away, along with some shovels and baskets, and a coil or two of rope; the strange, unusual, uncomfortable smell, and the cadaverous light; were all in unison. It was a cold and dismal scene.** Outside the realms of fiction it is also the church where Lord Byron was christened and where Robert Browning married Elizabeth Barrett.

The church is next door to the site of Dickens's second of three main London residences: 1 Devonshire Terrace. At the corner of Marylebone High Street is a frieze and a plaque on a modern building.

The frieze of 1962 by Estcourt J Clack illustrates characters that Dickens wrote about while he was based here, between 1839 and 1851, the years of *The Old Curiosity Shop, Barnaby Rudge, A Christmas Carol* and *David Copperfield*. The house had thirteen rooms and was at the end of a terrace. It had a garden at the end of which was a coach-house. Dickens kept a small pair of ponies, and hired a groom. He rented it all for £160 a year, and paid £800 for the last twelve years of the lease. In the 1841 census five servants are recorded as living here. Dickens described himself as "Gentleman". Mrs Gaskell visited him at this house and described his study: "There are books all round, up to the ceiling, and down to the floor."

When he was at work he insisted on absolute silence whereas when he was at leisure, in the words of his daughter, Mamie, "the bustle and noise of the great city became necessary to him." His study at Devonshire Terrace opened on to the garden but there was an extra baize door to enable him to keep out the noise as he worked. But the house became famous for the parties. **Such dinings**, he wrote to an American friend, Cornelius Felton, **such dancings, such conjurings, such blind-man's-buffings, such theatre-goings, such kissings out of old years and kissings-in of new ones, never took place in these parts before**. And to William Macready, his actor friend, then on tour in the United States, he wrote how he and his future biographer, John Forster, conjured bravely, that a plum-pudding was produced from an empty saucepan, **held over a blazing fire kindled in Stanfield's hat without damage to the lining; that a box of bran was changed into a live guinea-pig, which ran between my godchild's feet, and was the cause of such a shrill uproar and clapping of hands.**

In the garden Dickens used to keep ravens. One died and Dickens suspected that it had been poisoned. He arranged for an autopsy on the dead bird. Dickens's suspicions were unfounded and the cause of the raven's death was given as influenza. **He has left considerable property, chiefly in cheese and halfpence, buried in different parts of the garden. The new raven (I have a new one, but he is comparatively of weak intellect) administered to his effects, and turns up something every day. The last piece of *bijouterie* was a hammer of considerable size, supposed to have been stolen from a vindictive carpenter, who had been heard to speak darkly of vengeance ...** A later pet raven **died unexpectedly by the kitchen fire. He kept his eye to the last upon the meat as it roasted, and suddenly turned over on his back with a sepulchral cry of "Cuckoo!"** Dickens's ravens were the original models for Barnaby Rudge's pet, Grip.

Henry Wadsworth Longfellow visited him here in 1841. "The raven croaks in the garden," he wrote home from his host's study, "and the ceaseless roar of London fills my ears."

Dickens was happy here. **I seem as if I had plucked myself out of my proper soil when I left Devonshire Terrace,** he wrote in 1844 from Genoa where he lived for twelve months, **and would take root no more until I return to it.** When he lived at Devonshire Terrace Dickens was an occasional worshipper – or "took sittings" – at a nearby Unitarian Church in Little Portland Street.

The second on the right after Marylebone High Street brings us to Harley Street. Dickens did not like this street. **The expressionless uniform twenty houses,** Dickens wrote in *Little Dorrit,* **all to be knocked at and rung at in the same form, all approachable by the same dull steps, all fended off by the same pattern of railings, all with the same impracticable fire-escapes, the same inconvenient fixtures in their heads, and everything, without exception, to be taken at a high valuation ...**

His villains lived in streets in and around here. The swindling financier, Mr Merdle in *Little Dorrit*, lived in Harley Street. And four blocks to the south and parallel with Harley Street is Mansfield Street, where Mr Dombey had his house.

Mr Dombey's house was a large one, on a shady side of a tall, dark, dreadfully genteel street in the region between Portland Place and Bryanston Square. [It is much nearer Portland Place than Bryanston Square; and one might add that the literal shadiness depends on the time of day and position of the sun.] **It was a corner house, with wide areas containing cellars, frowned upon by barred windows, and leered at by crooked-eyed doors leading to dust-bins. It was a house of dismal state, with a circular back to it, containing a whole suit of drawing rooms looking upon a gravelled yard, where two gaunt trees, with blackened trunks and branches, rattled rather than rustled, their leaves were so smoke-dried.** The house to the west on the corner of Mansfield Mews has a yard that could be dismal – a high wall separates it from the road. The house opposite on the corner of Duchess Street has a semi-circular bay.

To the south is Cavendish Square. From here westward runs Wigmore Street where Madame Mantalini's dress-making establishment in *Nicholas Nickleby* was probably sited – number 11 has been suggested, though today Wigmore Place is where number 11 would be.

Along Wigmore Street we come to Wimpole Street on the right. Number 43 is believed to have been the residence of Mr and Mrs Boffin in *Our Mutual Friend* – **a corner house not far from Cavendish Square.** The house was later the property of Mr and Mrs John Harmon. Near here Silas Wegg had his stall.

Parallel to Wimpole Street further west is Welbeck Street. The building on the left, formerly number 64 and now Welbeck House, was the London residence of Lord George Gordon, the leader of the riots described in *Barnaby Rudge*.

Oxford Street is parallel to Wimpole Street to the south. If we walk along Oxford Street in a westerly direction, and turn left just at Bond Street Station, we head down Davies Street to Brook Street where, in *Dombey and Son*, the Fenix family had their town house. The Honorable Mrs Shrewton borrowed the house for her daughter's wedding to Mr Dombey.

Davies Street continues, passing (rich) Americans' favourite hotel, Claridge's. The hotel was founded in 1855 by an enterprising and resourceful former butler who bought an older hotel, Milvart's Hotel, on this site. It was probably Milvart's Hotel where Nicholas Nickleby paused for a pint of wine and a biscuit. **It was very handsomely furnished, the walls were ornamented with the choicest specimens of French paper enriched with a gilded cornice of elegant design. The floor was covered with a rich carpet, and two superb mirrors, one over the chimney-piece, the other reaching from floor to ceiling, multiplied the other beauties and added new ones of their own to enhance the general effect.** As Nicholas sipped the wine he overheard his sister being discussed in offensive terms by Sir Mulberry Hawk and a friend.

If we continue south to Berkeley Square and Berkeley Street, we reach Piccadilly. In the 1860s there used to be a hotel, St James's Hotel, at this corner. In 1869, the year before he died, Dickens came up from his Kent country house at Gad's Hill and stayed here for a few weeks in order to meet American friends and to be near a London doctor. In *Little Dorrit* Dickens described the area unsympathetically. **They rode to the top of Oxford Street, and, there alighting, dived in among the great streets of melancholy stateliness, and the little streets that try to be as stately and succeed in being more melancholy, of which there is a labyrinth near Park Lane. Wildernesses of corner-houses with barbarous old porticoes and appurtenances; horrors that came into existence under some wrong-headed person in some wrong-headed time, still**

demanding the blind admiration of all ensuing generations and determined to do so until they tumbled down. He really did not care for this area, Mayfair.

Devonshire House, one of the greatest of aristocratic houses – the London base of the Dukes of Devonshire – was located on the right, facing Piccadilly and the western edge of Green Park. It had been built in 1749 for the third Duke of Devonshire but was demolished in 1924. Here in May 1851 Dickens directed a play written by Bulwer Lytton, "Not so Bad as We Seem", in the presence of Queen Victoria and the Prince Consort. The Queen was amused.

Let us turn left along Piccadilly. On the eastern corner of Dover Street is the site of the coaching inn, the White Horse, the starting point for coaches to the west of England. Being in the fashionable and leisured West End of London people would gather to watch the departure of the evening coach. Itinerant peddlers used to gather to sell fruit and sponges for the passengers. The inn had a travellers' waiting room, **divided into boxes for the solitary confinement of travellers …[It] is furnished with a clock, a looking-glass, and a live waiter, which latter article is kept in a small kennel for washing glasses in a corner of the apartment.** From here Mr Pickwick and company set off for Bath. Sam Weller observed that the proprietor of the coach was another Pickwick. Sam thought this outrageous – **"An't nobody to be whopped for takin' this here liberty?"** It was also the destination of coaches from Reading, and here Esther Summerson in *Bleak House* first arrived in London, according to instructions. She was met at the Booking Office known as the White Horse Cellars, on the other side of the road, by Mr Guppy, who later referred to the first encounter when he proposed disastrously to her, referring to that first meeting at what he called **Whytorseller.**

If we walk up Piccadilly towards Piccadilly Circus we pass Albany (or The Albany – a very English controversy revolves around which is the correct form), which for two hundred years was a favoured home for well-connected bachelors. It is located opposite Fortnum and Mason's fifty yards up a gated road, the Albany Court Yard. Part of the lease is held by Peterhouse, one of the colleges of the University of Cambridge. Dickens's older literary and lordly contemporaries, Byron and Macaulay, had sets of chambers in (the) Albany. Dickens housed "Fascination" Fledgeby, in *Our Mutual Friend*, here.

Mr and Mrs Lammles, also of *Our Mutual Friend*, used, in their days of prosperity, to live in Sackville Street to the left.

Beyond Sackville Street and before Air Street on the left is the place where St James's Hall used to stand. The site is now occupied by le Meridien Hotel. It was here that Dickens used to give most of his London readings. He was always an actor manqué and he threw himself into dramatic readings. They both invigorated him and exhausted him. He was always punctiliously dressed. He was meticulous about all the arrangements – position of the lectern, lighting, the manner and style and timing of his entry on to the stage. He also made plenty of money to meet the commitments of his later years, providing for his separated wife, for wayward and feckless offspring as well as two of his own households, quite apart from a household for Ellen Ternan, his actress friend, and her family. His rendering of the death of Little Nell from *The Old Curiosity Shop* and the murder of Nancy from *Oliver Twist* made enormous physical and emotional demands both on Dickens himself, but no less on his audience. After giving his readings he rarely appeared for an encore. But in March 1870, frail and prematurely aged, he gave a farewell speech: **For some fifteen years, in this hall and many kindred places, I have had the honour of presenting my own cherished ideas before you for your recognition; and in closely observing your reception of them, have enjoyed an amount of artistic delight and enjoyment, which perhaps it is given to few men to know … . Ladies and gentlemen, in but two short weeks from this time, I hope that you may enter, in your own homes, on a new series of Readings, at** which my assistance will be indispensable; but from these garish lights I vanish now for ever, with one heartfelt, grateful, respectful, and affectionate farewell. (Dickens was alluding to the forthcoming serialisation of *The Mystery of Edwin Drood.*) After these words there was a dead silence as he turned away, deeply affected. Then, his daughter, Mamie, recalled, "such a burst and tumult of cheers and applause as were almost too much to bear." Within three months he was dead.

On the south side of Piccadilly, between the pedestrian Eagle Place and Piccadilly Circus, at no 193, were the premises of the publishers, Chapman and Hall, who brought out Dickens's earlier books, from *Pickwick Papers* to *Martin Chuzzlewit.*

If we cross to the north of Piccadilly Circus and go up Sherwood Street, cross Brewer Street and continue on Lower James Street, we reach Golden Square. At number 6, on the east side, is the presumed house of Ralph Nickleby. The site has probably been rebuilt more than once since the 1840s. There is no trace of a numbered building. Today the site is occupied by a construction of brick, stone and glass, the offices of a public relations agency. Dickens described Golden Square as **one of the squares that have been; a quarter of the town that has gone down in the world, and taken to letting lodgings. Many of its first and second floors are let, furnished, to single gentlemen, and it takes boarders besides. It is a great resort of foreigners.**

Carnaby Street that runs from south to north, one block to the north of Golden Square, was – at number 48 – the home of the Kenwigs family in *Nicholas Nickleby*. Number 48 is in an eighteenth century terrace house, now hosting a smart clothes shop. Another Nickleby connection is The Crown Inn, at the junction of Upper James Street and Beak Street. This was Newman Noggs's favourite watering hole. In his first letter to Nicholas, Newman Noggs wrote that **"they know where I live at the sign of the Crown, Golden**

Square". There is no Crown Inn today but an Old Coffee House with bars faces Upper James Street.

The prostitute in *Nicholas Nickleby*, Martha, also lived in this area, **in one of the sombre streets of which there are several in that part, where the houses were once fair dwellings, in the occupation of single families, but have, and had, long degenerated into poor lodgings let off in rooms.**

If we thread our way north, we reach Oxford Street. Dickens's maternal grandmother, former housekeeper of the Marquess of Crewe and possible model of Mrs Rouncewell, housekeeper at Chesney Wold in *Bleak House*, lived in Oxford Street, where Charles as a boy was brought to see her. Newman Street goes to the north. In this street, perhaps at number 26, Mr Turveydrop in *Bleak House* had his Dancing Academy – **in a sufficiently dingy house, at the corner of an archway.** Part of number 26 overhangs an arch that leads into Newman Passage. Here Mr Turverdrop occupied the best part of the house, with his son and daughter-in-law, formerly Caddy Jellaby, quartered in upper rooms, normally occupied by domestic staff.

A little further to the east, off Oxford Street on the south side, is Dean Street. Carlisle Street goes off on the left to join Soho Square. If we head south from the Square into Greek Street we reach Manette Street on the left, passing under an archway that is part of the Pillars of Hercules public house. Manette Street leads on to Charing Cross Road by Foyle's Bookshop. Having previously been Rose Street, the street was given this name in 1895 in honour of Dr Manette, the French refugee in *A Tale of Two Cities*. He had lived, not in this street, but perhaps in Carlisle Street. **A quieter corner than the corner where the Doctor lived was not to be found in London. There was no way through it, and the front window of the Doctor's lodgings commanded a pleasant little vista of street that had a congenial air of retirement on it. There were few buildings then,** north of the Oxford Road, and forest-trees flourished, and wild flowers grew, and the hawthorn blossomed, in the now vanished fields.

St Sepulchre's Church Holborn

From Bermondsey to Holborn Circus

The walk starts in Bermondsey and takes us to the City of London. Then, after another optional underground journey we move to Smithfield and Clerkenwell and to parts of London particularly associated with Oliver Twist.

BERMONDSEY has undergone several transformations since the 1830s. Slum clearances in the nineteenth century, extensive improvements during the twentieth century, and severe bomb damage during the Second World War have made it hard to trace the location of Jacob's Island where Bill Sikes in *Oliver Twist* made his last stand. He tried to lower himself from a building known as Metcalf Yard into a ditch with a rope attached to a chimney. But he lost his grip and hanged himself by the rope.

Near to that part of the Thames ... where the buildings on the banks are dirtiest, and the vessels on the river blackest, with the dust of colliers and the smoke of close-built, low-roofed houses. In such a neighbourhood, beyond Dockhead, in the borough of South- wark, stands Jacob's Island, surrounded by a muddy ditch, six or eight feet deep, and fifty or twenty wide when the tide is in, once called Mill Pond, but known in the days of this story as Folly Ditch.

A street called Dockhead is still there and Jacob Street perpetu-
ates the memory of the Island. Folly Ditch flowed into the Thames
through what is now Mill Street, a narrow road that resembles a
canyon between high buildings. The oldest building here is the Neo
Concordia Wharf, fronting on to St Saviour's Dock, created out of
one of the lost rivers of London, the Neckinger. Jacob's Island was
to the north of Wolseley Street, formerly London Street. Wooden
bridges over the sewer-infested canals led to the island and **crazy
wooden galleries, common to the backs of half-a-dozen houses**

used to ornament the banks of Folly Ditch. Dickens in the 1830s got to know the area when it was at its worst: **the filthiest, the strangest, the most extraordinary of the many localities that are hidden in London, wholly unknown, even by name, to the great mass of the inhabitants.** Cholera broke out here between 1849 and 1852 and there was a major fire in 1861. After that the area was demolished and the Victorian buildings replacing the slums have themselves been replaced. In the last twenty years there has been a further metamorphosis. Today the only water inland, away from the dock and the river is an ornamental pool, with fountain, in the gardens of Providence Square. The gardens are accessible only to the residents of the smart high-rise flats surrounding the gardens. A two-bedroom flat here goes for £525,000.

Dickens is commemorated in the blocks of flats in the area around, between Jamaica Road and the river. The blocks are named Brownlow, Tapley, Dombey, Copperfield, Nickleby, Bardell, Oliver, Pickwick, Weller, Tupman, Rudge, Micawber, Spenlow, Wickfield, Trotwood, Maylie, Oliver, Wrayburn, Havisham, Trotwood. All have been built in the 1950s.

We can walk westwards near the river. A footbridge crosses the St Saviour's Dock and a wide path, an esplanade, follows the river up to Tower Bridge. A string of smart wine bars and restaurants occupy the former wharves. One, with extraordinary pretentiousness, calls itself Le Pont de la Tour. ("Le Pont de la Tour combines traditional yet innovative French cuisine, knowledgeable and friendly staff, thoughtful design that evokes the Parisian chic of the 1930s, and glamorous views of the City and Tower Bridge.") The small smart pier opposite is Butler's Wharf Pier. It was around here that Quilp, in *The Old Curiosity Shop*, had *his* wharf, a **small, rat-infested, dreary yard, in which were a little wooden counting-house, burrowing all awry in the dust as if it had fallen from the clouds, and ploughed into the ground; a few fragments of rusty** anchors, several large iron rings, some piles of rotten wood, and two or three heaps of old sheet copper – crumpled, cracked, and battered.

Today it is possible to take Riverboat Disco Cruises from the pier.

Let us now cross the Thames by Tower Bridge – built in the 1890s – and pass the Tower of London on the left, built in the eleventh century by King William I (the Conqueror). We come to Tower Hill. Lord George Gordon, in *Barnaby Rudge*, was imprisoned in **a dreary room** in the Tower of London. And David Copperfield took his aunt, Betsey Trotwood, to see it. On the north-west side of Tower Hill, Mr Quilp in *The Old Curiosity Shop* is believed to have had his home, living there with his wife and his mother-in-law, Mrs Jiniwin.

A mile to the west of Tower Hill – two stops on the Underground from Tower Hill to Mansion House, from where there is a walk of two hundred yards – is Southwark Bridge. In *Little Dorrit*, this was Amy Dorrit's favourite walk. In that book it was known as the Iron Bridge. The present steel bridge was constructed in the 1920s, replacing an iron structure designed by John Rennie in 1814–19, who also designed the stone London Bridge. On Southwark Bridge Amy turned down the persistent proposal of John Chivery.

If we return to Mansion House station, and head westward along Cheapside, passing St Paul's Cathedral on the left, we see on the right the British Telecom Centre. Most of the constructions around here today replace buildings bombed during the Second World War. The British Telecom Centre appropriately replaces the Post Office. The bombed building had been built to a design of Robert Smirke in 1828, replacing a notorious slum. Smirke's building greatly impressed John Browdie, Nichlas Nickleby's Yorkshire friend. (Dickens took great efforts to reproduce authentically the Yorkshire dialect.)

"Wa-at dost thee ta' yon place to be, noo, that 'un ower the wa'?

Ye'd never coom near it, gin ye thried for twolve months. It's na but a Poast-office. Ho, ho! they need to charge for double lathers. A Poast-office! What dost thee think of that? Ecod, if that's on'y a Poast-office, I'd loike to see where the Lord Mayor o' London lives!"

A plaque on the western side of the building records the fact that, in 1896, Gugleilmo Marconi made the first transmission of radio signals here under the patronage of the chief engineer of the General Post Office.

To the north is the Barbican complex that includes the Museum of London. A network of overground walkways includes one called Falcon Highwalk. This is the only echo of Falcon Square where the Falcon Hotel was sited. This hotel was the base of John Jasper in *The Mystery of Edwin Drood* when he came to London from Cloisterham (Rochester).

It is hotel, boarding-house, or lodging-house at its visitor's option ... It bashfully, almost apologetically, gives the traveller to understand that it does not expect him, on the good old constitutional plan, to order a pint of sweet blacking for his drinking, and throw it away; but insinuates that he may have his boots blacked instead of his stomach, and may also have bed, breakfast, attendance, and a porter up all night, for a certain fixed charge.

The road going north from Aldersgate Underground station, heading for the Angel, Islington, is Goswell Street. This was Goswell Road in *Pickwick Papers* where Mr Pickwick rented rooms with Mrs Bardell. When he looked out of the window, **Goswell-street was at his feet, Goswell-street was on the right hand – as far as the eye could reach, Goswell-street extended on his left, and the opposite side of Goswell-street was over the way.** Today Goswell Road is an undistinguished minor artery. A few houses on the eastern side of the road have survived from the time of Mr Pickwick. Neither then nor now was Goswell Street a particularly fashionable place to live.

When at the beginning of the novel Mr Pickwick set off for Rochester, he walked the first mile to St Martin's-le-Grand from where he took a cab to the Golden Cross.

On the western side of Aldersgate, the road called Little Britain leads to Bartholomew Close. Mr Jaggers, in *Great Expectations*, had his offices here, assisted by Mr Wemmick. When Pip arrived here from Kent, he went for a turn in Smithfield, then the major meat market of the capital.

… I came into Smithfield; and the shameful place, being all asmear with filth, and fat, and blood, and foam, seemed to stick to me. So, I rubbed it off with all possible speed by turning into a street where I saw the great black dome of Saint Paul's bulging at me from behind a grim stone building which a bystander said was Newgate Prison.

Elsewhere in his journalism Dickens described Smithfield: The ground was covered, nearly ankle-deep, with filth and mire; a thick stream, perpetually rising from the reeking bodies of the cattle, and mingling with the fog, which seemed to rest upon the chimney-pots, hung heavily above. All the pens in the centre of the large area, and as many of the temporary pens as could be crowded into the vacant space, were filled with sheep; tied up to posts by the gutter-side were long lines of beasts and oxen, three or four deep. Countrymen, butchers, drovers, hawkers, boys, thieves, idlers, and vagabonds of every low grade, were mingled together in a dense mass. The whistling of drovers, the barking of dogs, the bellowing and plunging of oxen, the bleating of sheep, the grunting and squeaking of pigs; the cries of hawkers, the shouts, oaths, and quarrelling on all sides; the ringing of bells and the roaring of voices that issued from every public-house; the crowding, pushing, driving, beating, whooping, and yelling; the hideous and discordant din that resounded from every corner of the market; and the unwashed, unshaven, squalid, and dirty figures constantly running to and fro, and bursting in and out of the throng, rendered it a stunning and bewildering scene, which quite confounded the senses.

If we follow the pedestrianised part of Little Britain to the north we come to an open square – actually a circle – West Smithfield. From there we turn left, passing memorial tablets in the wall that commemorate first the Protestant martyrs who died in the reign of Queen Mary I in the 1550s, and then William Wallace, the Scottish leader executed here in 1305. (Film buffs will remember Mel Gibson's playing the part of Wallace in the 1995 film, *Braveheart*, and his desperate cry of "Freedom" as he died.) Following Giltspur Street we reach Newgate Street and face the Old Bailey, the Central Criminal Court, which took over the site of Newgate Prison. Newgate marked the western limits of the City of London. From Roman times there had actually been a gateway here.

Dickens wrote about this prison in four novels, *Barnaby Rudge*, *A Tale of Two Cities, Oliver Twist* and *Great Expectations*. A medieval prison was replaced in the 1770s with one designed by the architect, George Dance the Younger (who also designed both the southern front of the Guildhall and the Mansion House). This new prison was, within a few years of its construction, burnt to the ground in the Gordon riots of 1780, as described in *Barnaby Rudge*.

The prison was rebuilt and lasted until 1902, when it was pulled down and replaced by the present building.

From when it was rebuilt in 1783 until 1869 Newgate was the principal prison for serious criminals and was the scene of public executions. Before 1783 prisoners sentenced to death were placed in a cart and transported along Oxford Street to Tyburn, now occupied by Marble Arch, for a public hanging.

In *A Tale of Two Cities* the Old Bailey, which then included Newgate Prison, was the scene of the trial of Charles Darnay. The year is 1775 and Dickens described how the building was **a kind of deadly Inn yard, from which pale travellers set off continually, in carts and coaches, on a violent passage to the other world.... It was famous, too, for the pillory, a wise old institution that inflicted a punishment of which no one could foresee the extent; also for the whipping-post, another dear old institution, very humanising and softening to behold in action.**

Dickens was fascinated by prisons and was a frequent voyeuristic visitor here. He also included visits to prisons and penitentiaries (and morgues) whenever he travelled abroad, in mainland Europe and the United States. He was not a liberal prison reformer and in public presented a "tough" approach to the treatment of criminals. Above all, he argued in an article, "Lying Awake", in *Household Words* in 1852, let us have **no PET PRISONING, vain glorying, strong soup, and roasted meats, but hard work, and one unchanging and uncompromising dietary of bread and water, well or ill.** On the other hand he was able to empathise with prisoners. We remember Fagin in the condemned cell. On the morning of his execution, neighbouring windows **were filled with people, smoking and playing cards to beguile the time; the crowd were pushing, quarrelling and joking.** Meanwhile **the black stage, the cross-beam, the rope, and all the hideous apparatus of death** were ready for the public hanging.

In *Great Expectations*, Pip visits the prison. **We passed through the Lodge, where some fetters were hanging up ... It was visiting-time when Wemmick took me in, and a potman was going his rounds with beer, and the prisoners behind bars in yards were buying beer and talking to friends; and a frowsy, ugly, disorderly, depressing scene it was.**

On the northern side of the road is the church of St Sepulchre, just to the west of Giltspur Street. In the southern aisle are the remains of Captain John Smith, an early seventeenth-century

Governor of Virginia. There is also a Newgate Bell by a pillar in the southern aisle. This has a grim history. It was a legacy of 1605 that stipulated that whenever there was an execution, the bellman should give the bell twelve solemn double-strokes, outside the cell of the condemned. A poem was to be recited for the condemned men:

All you that in the condemned hole do lie,
Prepare you, for tomorrow you shall die.
Watch all, and pray: the hour is drawing near
That you before the Almighty must appear.
Examine well yourselves, in time repent,
That you may not to eternal flames be sent,
And when St Sepulchre's Bell in the morning tolls,
The Lord may have mercy on your souls.

To the west of St Sepulchre's Church the road used to descend sharply into the valley of the Fleet River. The old road went down to the right along Snow Hill. In the first paragraph of *Bleak House* Dickens imagines that, in the November mud, **it would not be wonderful to meet a Megalosaurus, forty feet long or so, waddling like an elephantine lizard up Holborn Hill.** The improvements of the 1860s when the Holborn Viaduct was built cleared away much slum property and also an old coaching inn, the Saracen's Head. In *Nicholas Nickleby*, this was the London base for Wackford Squeers for conducting business. He was too mean to stay there overnight. **What a vast number of random ideas there must perpetually be floating about regarding the name Snow Hill. The name is such a good one. Snow Hill, Snow – Hill, too, coupled with a Saracen's Head.** On entering the inn yard, **you will see the booking-office on your left, and the tower of St Sepulchre's Church, darting abruptly up into the sky, on your right, and a gallery of bedrooms**

on both sides. It was from here that Nicholas Nickleby set off with Squeers and some pupils for Greta Bridge by the Yorkshire coach. And here, in the same novel, John Browdie and his wife, with their bridesmaid, Fanny Squeers, arrived in London. He called it **Sarah's Son's Head.** (Mrs Nickleby called it, inconsequentially, **the Saracen with two necks.**) A police station is on the site of the old inn and a plaque records the memory of its predecessor, and fifty yards further north is an otherwise unmemorable construction with "Saracen's Head Buildings" carved in elegant nineteenth-century relief script.

Snow Hill leads down to Farringdon Road. If we head north for a third of a mile we reach the intersection of Clerkenwell Road. To the right is Clerkenwell Green (and the Marx Memorial Library). It is described in *Oliver Twist* as **an open square in Clerkenwell which is yet called by some strange perversion of terms The Green.**

A quarter of a mile to the north, Pear Tree Court, between Clerkenwell Close and Farringdon Lane, was a narrow court off the Green. Here Dickens located the bookshop where Mr Brownlow was absorbed in browsing through books on a stall outside. Oliver Twist was inveigled by the Artful Dodger and Charlie Bates into picking his pocket.

Pear Tree Court leads into Farringdon Road at the Betsey Trotwood public house, a watering hole that used to be popular with *Guardian* journalists – the offices of that paper were for twenty years across the road. The pub goes back to the 1860s and was built above the first underground railway line in London and was known as The Butcher's Arms until 1983 when it received its present name. Neither the pub nor the area has any connection with the great aunt of David Copperfield.

To the north is Exmouth Market, now a largely pedestrianised area. This used to be on the edge of the London's Italian quarter, "Little Italy", and at number 56 a plaque marks the home between

1818 and 1828 of Joseph Grimaldi (1778–1837), the son of an Italian father, one of the first Italian immigrants, and a British mother. Grimaldi developed the art of the clown, and introduced the Dame into pantomime. Dickens was a huge fan of Grimaldi and, after his death, edited a rambling manuscript that was the memoirs of "the prince of clowns". Dickens's work was creatively done. The original manuscript is lost but there are unmistakable Dickens touches. Dickens had happy memories of having seen Grimaldi in his prime and cheerfully undertook the work, at the same time as he was editing *Bentley's Miscellany* and writing *Oliver Twist*. But it was a work of love, and Dickens (aged twenty-five) got his father to help out in the task. Dickens acknowledged Grimaldi's professionalism, **his attention to his duties, and invariable punctuality ... perseverance and exertion.** These were qualities that marked Dickens himself. Grimaldi suffered from poverty and ended his life as a sad poverty-stricken alcoholic one mile to the north of Exmouth Market. At Rodney Street in Pentonville the former churchyard of St James's Church is now the Joseph Grimaldi Park. Dickens was acutely conscious of the need to be careful with money. His father's immurement in a debtor's prison was just one example to avoid. But two of his heroes, Grimaldi and Sir Walter Scott, in spite of their creative genius, also suffered acutely from financial problems. Their fate probably encouraged Dickens's own prudence and concern for due rewards for his work. It also explains his passionate support for copyright laws to ensure that writers, not printers and publishers, receive the financial rewards of creative work. On his first visit to the United States in 1842, Dickens loudly complained that America did not recognise international copyright conventions.

On the left of Farringdon Road, just beyond Exmouth Market is Mount Pleasant (Post) Sorting Office. This occupies the site of the House of Correction, formerly Cold Bath Prison, which Dickens also liked to visit.

We cross the route that Oliver Twist traversed on his first visit to London, as described in the novel. **Escorted by John Dawkins, they crossed from the "Angel" Inn into St John's-road; struck down the small street which terminates at Sadler's Wells Theatre; through Exmouth-street and Coppice Row; down the little court by the side of the workhouse; across the classic ground which once bore the name of Hockley-in-the-Hole; thence into Little Saffron-hill, and so into Saffron-hill the Great ... A dirtier or more wretched place he had never seen. The street was narrow and muddy; and the air was impregnated with filthy odours ... Covered ways and yards, which here and there diverged from the main street, disclosed little knots of houses, where drunken men and women were positively wallowing in the filth; and from several of the doorways, great ill-looking fellows were cautiously emerging: bound, to all appearance, on no very well-disposed or harmless errands.**

From Exmouth Street (as Exmouth Market used to be called) they would have turned left, south, crossed Farringdon Road and then right into Baker's Row and then south. Some of the names of streets have changed. The Workhouse has gone, but Little Saffron Hill is Crawford Passage leading to Herbal Hill, that leads to Clerkenwell Road, on the other side of which is Saffron Hill (no longer Great, not very hilly, and no longer growing the saffron that flourished there in the eighteenth century).

Just to the south of Clerkenwell Road and to the right off Saffron Hill is Hatton Wall. On the south of Hatton Wall stood the Metropolitan Police Court where Oliver Twist was taken to face charges of picking the pocket of Mr Brownlow in Pear Tree Court. Oliver **was led beneath a low archway and up a dirty court into this dispensary of summary justice, by the back way. It was a small paved yard into which they turned.** Mr Fang was the presiding magistrate of the court charging Oliver for theft. Fang was based on a Allan

Stewart Laing whose notoriously brutal methods of administering justice had been observed by Dickens.

In Saffron Hill nothing survives from the early nineteenth century but the name. We need to overwork our imaginations to understand what it was like in the 1830s, when Fagin had his den in this locality. Acres of slums were demolished with the building of the Viaduct in the 1860s – described by Professor Andrew Sanders as London's first flyover. Field Lane, even the name, has been wiped off the face of the earth. It used to link Saffron Hill with Snow Hill. But Dickens caught its character: **In its filthy shops are exposed for sale, huge bunches of second-hand silk handkerchiefs of all sizes and patterns, for here reside the traders who purchase them from the pickpockets.**

The One Tun public house on the corner of Greville Street and Saffron Hill claims to be the original of The Three Cripples, described in *Oliver Twist* as **a low public-house situate in the filthiest part of Little Saffron Hill; a dark and gloomy den, where a flaring gas-light burnt all day.** Inside the **ceiling was blackened, to prevent its colour from being injured by the flaring lamps; and the place was so full of dense tobacco smoke that at first it was scarcely possible to discern anything more.** The public house was frequented by Sikes, Fagin and Monks. It was where Noah Claypole (alias Mr Morris Bolter), on his arrival in London, met Fagin. Today the One Tun, built in 1875, provides Thai food but disallows customers who might have "dirty boots or soiled clothing".

The Saffron Hill district, the headquarters of Fagin's organised crime in the 1830s, was a century later the area of operations for another organised criminal gang, "the Italian mob", the leaders of whom were the Sabini brothers. Their gang leader, Charles, was known as "Darby" and was possibly the model for Colleoni in *Brighton Rock* by Graham Greene.

Saffron Hill at the southern end emerges on to High Holborn, to the west of the Viaduct. The Viaduct overshadows St Andrew's Church, built by Sir Christopher Wren, gutted in the Second World War and rebuilt since. When Bill Sikes took Oliver Twist to force an entry into the house at Chertsey, they passed the church **hard upon seven.** Its bells told David Copperfield he was a quarter of an hour late when he was due to call on Agnes Wickfield at the house of Mr Waterbrook in Ely Place.

Bleeding Heart Yard (the name alludes to a deer, a hart, that was wounded) lies parallel to Charterhouse Street and is tucked away behind St Etheldreda's Church. In *Little Dorrit* the Yard was the location of Arthur Clennam's family factory, Messrs Doyce and Clennam, and also the home of Mr and Mrs Plornish in the same novel. Today it is occupied by bistro restaurants and a repair shop for jewellery and watches. The craft of watch repairing was a speciality of the early Italian immigrants and of Clerkenwell to the east. Immediately to the west is Hatton Garden, centre of London's diamond trade.

If we walk down Hatton Garden to Holborn Circus and turn left and left again we find ourselves in Ely Place, a surviving gated street. In Dickens's time there were many such streets, including Doughty Street, his home in the late 1830s. David Copperfield met up with his old school chum, Tommy Traddles here at a dinner party attended also by Agnes Wickfield and Uriah Heep.

An equestrian statue of a hat-raising Prince Consort (the husband of Queen Victoria and an admirer of Charles Dickens) is in the centre of Holborn Circus. On the south side, between St Andrew Street and New Fetter Lane, is Thavies Inn House, the residence – at number 13 – of Mrs Jellyby and her disorderly and dysfunctional family, mercilessly satirised in *Bleak House*. Dickens described the street as a **narrow street of high houses like an oblong cistern to hold the fog.** Esther Summerson and Ada stayed here on their first night in London, and it was in the railings outside the house where the infant Peepy Jellyby caught her head in the railings, perhaps at a site now occupied by Pizza Express.

Remains of Marshalsea prison

From the Bank of England to Trafalgar Square via Southwark and Westminster

The last walk takes us from the City of London through parts of London south of the river, by the prisons associated with Dickens. We are in areas particularly associated with **Little Dorrit***. We pass by the grave of Dickens in Westminster Abbey.*

THE HEADQUARTERS of the firm of Dombey and Son was close to the Bank of England: a **magnificent neighbour; with its vaults of gold and silver.**

If we walk, the Bank of England, south-east along Lombard Street, past Hawksmoor's early eighteenth-century church of St Mary Wolnoth, we come to the church of Edmund King and Martyr on the left. Just past that is George Yard, which opens to a square. On the north-east corner is the George and Vulture Inn. This pub, today an eating and drinking centre for bankers and yuppies, is nearly always crowded. It can trace its history back to the twelfth century, when it was just called The George. Vulture was added later, certainly by the fifteenth century when the poet, John Skelton, wrote about it. The present building dates to the eighteenth century. It provided a base and residence – **good, old-fashioned and**

comfortable quarters – for Mr Pickwick after he had been obliged to leave Goswell Street, following the case of Bardell vs Pickwick. The walls of the downstairs rooms are covered with old prints of Dickens novels, and a copy of Maclise's 1839 portrait of Dickens. An upper room is called Mr Pickwick's Room where descendants of Charles Dickens meet each Christmas. On one of my visits, Fernando, the Columbian-born waiter, pointed out where Prince William, where Timothy Dalton and where Chris Eubank sat on their visits to the restaurant. But not at the same time.

Dickens's first love, Maria Beadnell, lived with her family at number 2, Lombard Street. Her father was manager of Smith, Payne and Smith's Bank at number 1. And in Lombard Street, the **golden street of the Lombards**, William Dorrit, newly released from the Marshalsea, met the speculator, Mr Merdle.

Lombard Street leads to Gracechurch Street. If we turn left we find on the right Bull's Head Passage which takes us to the site of the Green Dragon Tavern, which, it is believed, was The Blue Boar in *Pickwick Papers*. Here it was that Sam Weller wrote his Valentine (or **"Walentine"**) to his future wife, the pretty housemaid, Mary.

If we continue north along Gracechurch Street and turn left into Cornhill we come to Newman's Court on the right. In *Pickwick Papers* Dickens located the offices of the scheming lawyers, Dodson and Fogg, in Freeman's Court, Cornhill. There is a Freeman's Court off Cheapside but not in Cornhill, and it is believed that Dickens had Newman's Court here in mind. There are no entries to offices and most of the building is post-Pickwick, but there is an atmosphere of seedy shabbiness that would be appropriate to the world of Dodson and Fogg.

In *A Christmas Carol* Scrooge's counting house was around Cornhill and on the hill of Cornhill Bob Cratchit went **down into a slide in honour of its being Christmas Eve.**

Doubling back and crossing Gracechurch Street we come into Leadenhall Street. Number 157 was the House of Sol Gills in *Dombey and Son*, where Captain Cuttle was in charge – in Sol Gills's absence – of the ships' instrument makers. Over the door there had been an image of the **Wooden Midshipman; eternally taking observations of the hackney coaches.** A ships' instruments maker occupied these premises almost until the end of the nineteenth century. Today the plate glass offices of Tokio Marine Europe occupy the site.

We reach St Mary Axe Street, named after a church that was pulled down in the sixteenth century. In this street the good Jew, Riah, in *Our Mutual Friend* (created to offset the unfavourable impression left by Oliver Twist's bad Jew, Fagin) had his home and office, **a yellow overhanging plaster-fronted house.** Nothing survives from the nineteenth century. On the right we find one of twenty-first century London's most iconic structures, number 30, the Swiss Re Building, but known, from its shape and colour, as the Gherkin, designed by Norman Foster and Arap.

St Mary Axe leads on to Bevis Marks, where, at No 10, was the house of Sampson Brass and his sister, Sally, who was the more effective, if unofficial partner in, the legal business in *The Old Curiosity Shop*. Here lived their assistant, Dick Swiveller, and also the maid of all work, the Marchioness. Dickens wrote to his biographer, John Forster, describing how he **went to look for a house for Sampson Brass. But I got mingled up in a kind of social paste with the Jews of Houndsditch, and roamed about among them till I came out in Moorfields quite unexpectedly.** The office was **so close upon the footway, that the passenger who rakes the wall brushes the dim glass with his coat sleeve – much to its improvement, for it is very dirty.** Mr Richard, in the same novel, used to frequent the Red Lion inn on the northern side, long since gone.

If we continue south and then swing to the east, we pass Aldgate underground railway station. Just beyond the station on the left we are at the site of Bull Inn Yard, from where coaches set off for East Anglia. Mr Pickwick set off from here for Ipswich, the coachman in charge being Sam Weller's father, Tony. They set off and rattled along the Whitechapel Road **to the admiration of the whole population of that pretty densely-populated quarter.** There is no trace of this inn – no plaque, no surviving name – but, appropriately, on the other side of the road is a bus station with the successors of the coach and horses taking people not to East Anglia but to all parts of London.

Back at the road junction we turn left into Aldgate which leads on to Fenchurch Street. At the junction of that street and Leadenhall

Street is the Aldgate Pump, to which Mr Toots in *Dombey and Son* made regular excursions to get away from the happiness of Sol Gills.

Mincing Lane is the fifth road on the left. A building on the left, by Dunster Court, is claimed to be where Messrs Chicksey, Veneering and Stobbles had their druggist stores in *Our Mutual Friend*. R Wilfer, in the same novel, had his office next door.

In 1860, Dickens wrote a piece, later published in *The Uncommercial Traveller*, about churches in the City of London. He wrote about distinctive smells in the churches in this area ... **about Mark-lane, for example, there was a dry whiff of wheat; and I accidentally struck an airy sample of barley out of an aged hassock in one of them. From Rood-lane to Tower-street, and thereabouts, there was often a subtle flavour of wine; sometimes, of tea. One church near Mincing-lane smelt like a druggist's drawer. Behind the Monument the service had a flavour of damaged oranges, which, a little further down towards the river, tempered into herrings, and gradually toned into a cosmopolitan blast of fish.**

Turning right into Great Tower Street we reach its continuation, Eastcheap, off the left of which is Fish Street Hill. Just past the Monument, (which Mrs F's crazy aunt, in *Little Dorrit*, says, quite correctly, **"was put up arter the Great Fire of London"**) we come to the site of King's Head Court, **a small paved yard**, on the south side of which was Mrs Todgers's Commercial Boarding-House, celebrated at the Pecksniff's London base in *Martin Chuzzlewit*.

Right and then left, we are now at London Bridge. On the southwest side of the bridge there used to be a wide flight of steps leading down to the river. These were Nancy's Steps, commemorated in *Oliver Twist*. **The steps ... are on the Surrey bank and on the same side of the bridge as St Saviour's Church. [They] form a landing-stair from the river ... These steps are a part of the bridge; they consist of three flights. Just below the end of the second, going down, the stone wall on the left terminates in an ornamental**

pilaster facing towards the Thames. Nancy met Rose Maylie here, betraying Sikes and Fagin. Noah Claypole eavesdropped on the conversation and passed on what he heard to Fagin and Sikes, a betrayal that led to Bill Sikes murdering Nancy.

The bridge at the time *Oliver Twist* was written had only recently been built, replacing others that went back to the early Middle Ages. The then bridge had been designed by Sir John Rennie, and opened by King William IV in August 1831. It was replaced in the 1960s by the present construction. Rennie's bridge was dismantled and re-erected at Lake Havasu City, Arizona. The bridge included what used to be known as Nancy's Steps. Today there is a flight of steps on the west side of the bridge leading down to Tooley Street. These are erroneously known as Nancy's Steps. Indeed until a year ago there was a plaque on the wall stating this, and that Nancy was murdered here. In the 1960 musical, *Oliver!* by Lionel Bart, Nancy is killed here but this is pure fiction. It is a deviation from *Oliver Twist.*

The first chapter of *Our Mutual Friend* opens with Lizzie Hexam and her father on a boat, floating **on the Thames, between Southwark Bridge, which is of iron, and London Bridge, which is of stone, as an autumn evening was closing in.** Both bridges were designed by John Rennie, but Southwark Bridge was replaced in the early twentieth century. Amy Dorrit was fond of walking over Southwark Bridge, which was then a toll bridge. **"If you go by the Iron Bridge,"** she said, **"there is an escape from the noise of the street."**

We are now on what, in Dickens's time, was known as the Surrey side of the river. The borough of Southwark, at the beginning of the nineteenth century housed no fewer than seven of London's prisons. The borough also had some of the worst slums in all London.

In this neighbourhood, **in a by-street in Southwark, not far from London Bridge**, but today impossible to identify further because of comprehensive developments, was the home of the mother of Barnaby Rudge. Southwark Cathedral, formerly the parish church of St Saviour's, to the south-west of London Bridge, used to have some almshouses next to its Lady Chapel. In *David Copperfield*, Mell, the usher at Salem House School, used to go and visit his mother in almshouses, described in the novel as by London Bridge. The almshouses were probably demolished with the construction of the railway bridge leading to London Bridge Station to the east in 1849. Dickens regularly used this station on his frequent trips to France. In 1850 the journey took twelve hours. In the early seventeenth century the name of one of the prosperous families of Southwark was Harvard. John Harvard was baptised in this parish church. He later migrated to America and was the founder of Harvard University.

If we walk on along under the railway bridge and past St Thomas's Street and King's Head Yard on the left we come to White Hart Yard. This marks the site of one of several old taverns that lined the eastern side of the road. The inn could trace its history back to 1400. The white hart was the emblem of King Richard II who died in 1399. The inn flourished in the early nineteenth century and the building Dickens knew had been built after a fire in the 1670s. A balustrade of the inn has been preserved and is housed in the Dickens Museum in Doughty Street. Otherwise only the name is left of the inn, described in *Pickwick Papers* as one of half a dozen old inns having **preserved its external features unchanged, and which has escaped alike the rage for public improvement and the encroachments of private speculation. Great, rambling, queer old places they are, with galleries and passages and staircases, wide enough and antiquated enough to furnish materials for a hundred ghost stories.** It was at the White Hart that Sam Weller was working cleaning the boots of guests when Mr Pickwick recruited him as his personal servant. The sales of the serially produced *Pickwick Papers* shot up phenomenally, from 400 an issue to 40,000 an issue, once

Sam Weller was introduced into the story. That encounter and its literary consequences established Dickens as a best-selling author for the rest of his life. And it was at the White Hart Inn that Mr Alfred Jingle, having eloped with Rachel Wardle, ended up.

The White Hart Inn was demolished in 1889. But there are traces of other old taverns. The King's Head was destroyed late in the nineteenth century, but a King's Head Yard leads to the New King's Head. The names of the Queen's Head, the Talbot, the Three Tuns and the Tabard can be identified by Yard or plaque. It was from the Tabard that Chaucer's pilgrims set off for Canterbury in 1386. Three taverns are still in operation. The George is still flourishing and, with its balconies overlooking a yard, gives some idea of what the White Hart must have looked like. The others, a little further south, are St Christopher's and the Blue-Eyed Maiden.

Further along the Borough, we come to Southwark Public Library, named after John Harvard. A plaque celebrates the Harvard connection with Southwark. The alley just past the library is Angel Place, a name that recalls another old inn. On the right is an information board and some artwork indicating that this was the site of Marshalsea Prison. (Marshalsea Road opposite is a later misleading denomination; the road was not built until the 1880s.) Here Dickens's father was imprisoned for debt for three months in 1824, when Dickens was twelve years old. A few yards up Angel Place the brick wall on the right is all that is left of the prison. **Whoever goes into Marshalsea Place, turning out of Angel Court, leading to Bermondsey, will find his feet on the very paving-stones of the extinct Marshalsea jail; will see its narrow yard to the right, and to the left, very little altered if at all, except that the walls were lowered when the place got free; will look upon the rooms in which the debtors lived; and will stand among the crowding ghosts of many miserable years.**

While he was in the prison, John Dickens continued to receive his Navy Board salary, and was joined by his family who were free, during the day, to come in and out to see him. There was even a maid who came to look after him. John, a gregarious and social character, was chairman of a committee of prisoners, arranging social events.

When Dickens wrote *David Copperfield* his father was still alive. Wilkins Micawber, it is generally accepted, is partly based on John Dickens. The high spirits, the financial irresponsibility, the formal way he spoke and wrote, are all traits copied from his father. But it would have been too painful for Dickens to have described the humiliating years when his father was in Marshalsea prison, so Micawber, when he is in prison, is at the King's Bench prison a quarter of a mile away. The description of the King's Bench Prison is perfunctory. But by the time he wrote *Little Dorrit* his father was dead and he expanded himself in his descriptions of the Marshalsea.

Indeed Little Dorrit is remembered in the area. She was born in the Marshalsea and baptised in St George's Church, built in the 1730s, just beyond Angel Place. A turnkey was a godfather. As a little girl, one night Little Dorrit was too late to get back into the Marshalsea Prison and found shelter in the church vestry. Later on she was married here to Arthur Clennam. The east window has a small stained glass representation of Little Dorrit. Across the road can be found a Little Dorrit Court leading to a Little Dorrit playground. It has considerably improved since Dickens described the area:

... all the busy sounds of traffic resound in it from morn to midnight, but the streets around are mean and close; poverty and debauchery lie festering in the crowded alleys, want and misfortune are pent up in the narrow prison; an air of gloom and dreariness seems, in my eyes at least, to hang about the scene, and to impart to it a squalid and sickly hue.

If we head off to the south-west of the Borough, the first road on the right is Lant Street, which used to one of the **mean and close** streets, **a ganglion of roads**, as Dickens described them. **The majority** of the inhabitants [of Lant Street] **either direct their energies to the letting of furnished apartments, or devote themselves to the healthful and invigorating pursuit of mangling.** Half way along on the left is the Charles Dickens Primary School; it has also taken over the street, turning it into part of the school playground. The school is around the site of a house that Dickens occupied as a boy, while he worked at the blacking factory near Charing Cross and his father was in Marshalsea Prison. Rather than walk back to Camden Town each evening he preferred to find accommodation near his father. **An attic was found for me at the house of an insolvent-court agent, who lived in Lant Street, in the borough ... A bed and bedding were sent over for me, and made up on the floor. The little window had the pleasant prospect of a timber-yard; and when I took possession of my new abode, I thought it was a Paradise.** Just over ten years later, in *Pickwick Papers*, he has the medical student, Bob Sawyer, living there. It was appropriately near Guy's Hospital. **There is an air of repose about Lant Street, in the borough, which sheds a gentle melancholy upon the soul. A house in Lant Street would not come within the denomination of a first-rate residence, in the strict acceptation of the term; but it is a most desirable spot, nevertheless.** The residents, Dickens said, were **migratory, mostly disappearing on the verge of quarter-day, and generally by night. His Majesty's revenues are seldom collected in this happy valley; the rents are dubious; and the water communication is very frequently cut off.** There are today only two residential houses in the street, but next to the school stands a salubrious block of flats. The other buildings are warehouses or office premises, though there is a pub, the Gladstone Arms, named after that other iconic Victorian figure, the Prime Minister, Mr Gladstone.

The streets in the area were, in Dickens's time, among the poorest and most depressed in the capital. Such districts were where penurious migrants to the rapidly expanding capital settled in vile

lodging-houses. Mint Street, parallel to Lant Street, had the reputa-
tion of being one of the very worst streets in the 1840s. In the words
of John Hollingshead, writing in 1861, "We seem to have left civilisa-
tion behind us." Dickens had a curious fascination with slums and
used to take friends to look at them. Peter Ackroyd has suggested it
was "something very close to a spectator sport". In 1842 he brought
his American house-guest, Henry Wadsworth Longfellow, to Mint
Street. They went with Dickens's friends, the artist Daniel Maclise
and his future biographer, John Forster, and had the precaution of
a police escort. Maclise found the experience too horrific and was
unable to cope with the stench and filth. In 1851 Dickens accompanied one of the early London police detectives, Inspector Field, here.
He wrote the experiences up for *Household Words*. The street is **full
of low lodging-houses, as you see by the transparent canvas-lamps
and blinds, announcing beds for travellers.**

Later in the nineteenth century, these slums were replaced by the
Peabody buildings that exist to this day. George Peabody, a wealthy
American from Baltimore who settled in London, was appalled by
the grim housing and set up the Peabody Trust to provide "improved
model dwellings for the respectable working class". Some of the
streets have been named – we now have a Weller Street, a Pickwick
Street, a Copperfield Street and a Clennam Street.

To the south of Newington Causeway can be found the Inner
London Sessions House. To the east of the Sessions House is Harper
Road. The gardens behind the Sessions House – containing tennis
courts and a play area for young children – mark the site of the
Horsemonger Lane Gaol, built in 1791 and demolished ninety years
later. The poet, Leigh Hunt (to be guyed as Harold Skimpole in
Bleak House), was imprisoned here between 1812 and 1814 for libel-
ling the Prince Regent. During his confinement he was visited by
other poets, Lord Byron and Thomas Moore. There is no longer a
Horsemonger Lane, though the name is preserved in Horsemonger

Mews two blocks to the east. The gaol was replaced by these gardens, laid out by the Metropolitan Public Gardens Association and opened to the public in 1884 by Mrs Gladstone, wife of the Prime Minister of the time.

In November 1849 Dickens attended the public execution of a couple called Manning for the murder of one of their friends whose body they then buried under the kitchen floor. (**"I never liked him,"** Dickens quoted Manning as saying, **"and I beat in his skull with the ripping chisel."**) Houses across the road – since demolished – were let out so people could witness the hanging from the balconies. Dickens himself paid ten guineas for a ringside view. He was horrified and wrote a moving account of the execution in a letter to *The Times*. **When the two miserable creatures who attracted all this ghastly sight about them, were turned quivering in the air, there was no more emotion, no more pity, no more thought that two immortal souls had gone to judgment.** His letters were reprinted as handbills. Three years later, in an article in *Household Words* the memory still haunted him (**... those two forms dangling on the top of the entrance gateway – the man's, a limp, loose suit of clothes as if the man had gone out of them; the woman's, a fine shape, so elaborately corseted and artfully dressed, that it was quite unchanged in its trim appearance as it slowly swung from side to side ...**). The letters and article launched a campaign for the ending of public executions – the last taking place in 1868. Horsemonger Gaol was demolished in 1880 but the grave markers for the Mannings are now in the Cuming Museum in Walworth Road. Mrs Manning is believed to be the model for Hortense, the French maid of Lady Dedlock in *Bleak House*.

Today, diagonally opposite to the gardens, is the Baitul Aziz mosque, alongside Dickens Square.

In *Little Dorrit* Mr Chivery kept a tobacconist's shop in Horsemonger Lane, his customers being not only the general public but also prisoners. In the novel it is described as a **rural establishment one storey high, which had the benefit of the air from the yards of Horsemonger Lane Jail, and the advantage of a retired walk under the wall of that pleasant establishment.** His son, John, nursed an unrequited passion for Little Dorrit and sat in the backyard of the house, anticipating his death and composing woeful epitaphs for himself.

The north side of the junction of the Borough and Newington Causeway, just past Stones End Street, is where the King's Bench Prison for debtors used to be. Debtors were permitted to leave the prison and circulate within "the rules" of the prison. The rules was an area, sometimes called a liberty, **adjoining the prison, and comprising some dozen streets in which debtors who could raise money to pay large fees, from which their creditors do *not* derive any benefit, are permitted to reside.** Here Mr Micawber in *David Copperfield* was detained in the prison and arranged to meet David and Tommy Traddles (**D.V.**) **on the outside of the south wall of that place of incarceration on civil process.** Inside the prison life was relaxed for the prison had all sorts of facilities, including reading rooms, a fives court and up to thirty gin shops.

If we turn west and go along Borough Road we come to St George's Circus. An obelisk stands in the middle of this junction of six roads. Erected in 1771, it records the distances to Fleet Street, Palace Yard Westminster and London Bridge. When David Copperfield was about to walk to Dover to see his aunt, Betsey Trotwood, he arranged for **a long-legged man with a very little empty donkey-cart** to take his possessions wrapped in a box to Dover for sixpence. He handed over the box and never saw it again.

At the beginning of Blackfriars Road and on the left there used to be the Surrey Theatre, where Little Dorrit's sister, Fanny, was a dancer while her uncle, Frederick, played **a clarionet as dirty as himself** in the orchestra. The theatre has been replaced by McLaren House, part of the South Bank University. A small plaque commemorates, not the theatre nor Fanny Dorrit, but the deaths of eleven London firemen who were killed by enemy action while relaying water from the basement of the former theatre, which had been pulled down in 1934 having served as a cinema and a scenery paint shop.

On the opposite road, heading south-west, Lambeth Road, in extensive parkland gardens, is the Imperial War Museum. The museum was founded during the First World War and took over buildings previously occupied by the old Bethlehem Hospital, known as Bedlam, for the mentally afflicted, the history of which went back to the Middle Ages. Much of the central part of the building, including the impressive dome and six-column portico, was built in 1838–40 to the design of Sydney Smirke. It was still a mental hospital in Dickens's time. In an article he wrote for *All the Year Round* in 1860, he reflected: **Are not the sane and the insane equal at night as the sane lie a dreaming? Are not all of us outside this hospital, who dream more or less in the condition of those inside it, every night of our lives?**

Two blocks to the south of the Imperial War Museum is Walcot Square. On his second proposal to Esther Summerson in *Bleak House* Mr Guppy declared that one of his assets was **"a house in that locality, which, in the opinion of my friends, is a hollow bargain (taxes ridiculous, and use of fixtures included in the rent) ... It's a six-roomer, exclusive of kitchens,"** said Mr Guppy, **"and in the opinion of my friends, a commodious tenement."** Walcot Square, built in 1837–39, still survives, and was perhaps a social advance on Mr Guppy's previous lodgings in Pentonville when he made his first offer of marriage.

We head westward to the roundabout before Lambeth Bridge, where we turn right along Lambeth Bridge Road, past the church, now a Gardening Museum, and past Lambeth Palace, the official residence of the Archbishops of Canterbury. We sweep away from the river with, on the left, St Thomas's Hospital. After that we come to another large roundabout. Left leads us to Westminster Bridge. A Florence Nightingale Museum on the left is roughly on the site of Astley's Theatre, demolished in 1896. It was here that Christoper ("Kit") Nubbles, in *The Old Curiosity Shop*, used to come to a performance once every three months when he had received his quarterly salary. And in *Bleak House* Trooper George came here and was **much delighted with the horses and feats of strength; looks at the weapons with a critical eye; disapproves of the combats, as giving evidence of unskilful swordsmanship; but is touched home by the sentiments.**

If we double back along the Lambeth Bridge Road and cross the Thames by Lambeth Bridge, we come to Millbank. There used to be a large penitentiary facing the river, on the site of which today stands the Tate Gallery. David Copperfield and Mr Peggotty searched the area for the fallen Martha, **near the great blank prison.**

Proceeding north, we come to Dean Stanley Street that takes us to Smith Square. Jenny Wren, the Dolls' Dressmaker in *Our Mutual Friend*, lived in this street, formerly Church Street. Lizzie Hexam also lodged here between the death of her father and her marriage to Eugene Wrayburn. Dickens's view of St John's Church, Smith Square, would not be echoed by many today: **In this region are a certain little street called Church Street, and a certain little blind square called Smith Square, in the centre of which last retreat is a very hideous church, with four towers at the four corners, generally resembling some petrified monster, frightful and gigantic, on its back with its legs in the air.** The crippled Jenny Wren was teased for her disability by children. Her revenge was to push them in the church crypt. **"I'd cram 'em all in, and then I'd lock the door and through the key hole I'd blow in pepper."** The church, built between 1713 and 1728, is today famous for regular concerts and the crypt has been transformed into a restaurant, popular with parliamentarians.

Millbank leads by Abingdon Street to Old Palace Yard, with St Stephen's Tower on the right – part of the buildings of parliament, known as the Palace of Westminster. In *Our Mutual Friend* Julius Handford, alias John Harmon, gave as his address The Exchequer Coffee House, Palace Yard, Westminster.

The present buildings of the Houses of Parliament were erected after the old buildings were destroyed by fire in 1834. Dickens's father had been a reporter here, transcribing debates for the record. When he was only twenty, Dickens was introduced by his father to the same work. Dickens had already taught himself shorthand and immediately became a star reporter, making, as he later put it, **quite a splash**. The parliamentary Reform Act of 1832 was the first step towards a parliament that was more representative of the people, and the first election after the reform returned a galaxy of parliamentary and intellectual talent: Sir Robert Peel, Lord John Russell, William Cobbett, Daniel O'Connell, Lord Stanley ("the Rupert of Debate"), and of a young generation, Macaulay and Gladstone. But Dickens, strangely, was unimpressed and professed a **hatred of the falseness of talk, of bombastic eloquence.** In 1841 he declined an invitation to stand as a Radical Liberal candidate for Reading – his friend, lawyer and playwright and dedicatee of *Pickwick Papers*, Sir Thomas Talfourd, was already a Member of Parliament for that borough.

Westminster Hall, the cavernous barn-like structure, that dates back to the eleventh century and was spared the fire of 1834, housed law courts from the thirteenth century until 1882. One was the Court of Chancery and it was here in *Bleak House* that the final verdict of the Jarndyce vs Jarndyce case was concluded. Here too Lord George Gordon was tried for High Treason – and acquitted – in *Barnaby Rudge*. Dickens was twenty-one, when his first story, "A Dinner at Poplar Walk", was accepted for publication by *Monthly Magazine*. When he heard the news of his first publication, **I walked down to Westminster-hall, and turned into it for half an hour, because my** eyes were so dimmed with joy and pride that they could not bear the street, and were not fit to be seen there.

To the left lies Westminster Abbey, with St Paul's Cathedral, one of the two major churches of the capital. In it rest the bodies of kings and queens, statesmen and soldiers. One area in the south transept is set aside for the graves of artists and writers – Poets' Corner. The first poet to be buried here was Geoffrey Chaucer in 1400 – and the last was an actor, Laurence Olivier. Charles Dickens was buried here near to the dramatist, Robert Brinsley Sheridan, and the actor, David Garrick, on 14 June 1870. Dickens had wanted to be buried in Rochester Cathedral, but the graveyard there was closed for further burials.

Dickens died of cerebral haemorrhage on Friday, 9 June 1870. On the following Monday, *The Times* thundered that only Westminster Abbey would be fitting to receive a writer of such distinction. Later on the same morning Dean Stanley, after whom Church Street was later renamed and the clergyman in charge of all that went on in the Abbey, had a visit from one of Dickens's sons and his biographer, John Forster. They explained that if Dickens was to be buried in the Abbey, it had to be a modest and private burial early in the morning. So the body was brought by train from Rochester to Charing Cross station on the morning of Wednesday 14 June and three mourning coaches and the hearse came to the Abbey. There was none of what Dickens's old newspaper, *The Daily News*, called "the dismal frippery of the undertaker". The only attendants were his immediate family, his doctor, his solicitor, and two friends – John Forster and the novelist Wilkie Collins.

It was all over quite early and when later in the morning a journalist asked the Dean about the funeral he replied, "It has already taken place." The grave was left open for the rest of the day, and the spot was visited by thousands of mourners, many of whom strewed flowers over the plain but polished oak coffin. In the following days many thousands also came to pay their respects.

Parliament Street, leading to Whitehall, exits Parliament Square to the north at the north-east corner. In Derby Gate, on the left, is The Red Lion, where Dickens, aged twelve, and with money in his pocket, asked the landlord for a drink.

"What is your very best, the VERY *best* – ale a glass?" …

"Twopence," says he.

"Then," says I, "just draw me a glass of that if you please, with a good head to it."

The landlord looked at me, in return over the bar, from head to foot, with a strange smile on his face, and instead of drawing the beer, looked round the screen and said something to his wife, who came out from behind it, with her work in her hand, and joined him in surveying me … They asked me a good many questions, as to what my name was, how old I was, where I lived, how I was employed, etc., etc. To all of which, that I might commit nobody, I invented appropriate answers. They served me with the ale, though I suspect it was not the strongest on the premises; and the landlord's wife, opening the little half-door and bending down, gave me a kiss that was half-admiring and half-compassionate, but all womanly and good, I am sure.

The story, without a reference to the inn, was replicated in *David Copperfield*.

As we continue along Whitehall we pass the Horse Guards, with two horsemen in nineteenth-century military dress at the gates. We can walk through the Horse Guards to Horse Guards Parade, where the Queen "troops the colour" on her official birthday in June each year. St James's Park lies beyond. On the eastern side, Martin Chuzzlewit arranged to meet Mary Graham just before his departure to the United States. The rendezvous had been orchestrated by Martin's servant, Mark Tapley, who timed it precisely according to the clock on the Horse Guards.

If we pass through Admiralty Arch at the north-east end of The

Mall, turn left into Spring Gardens, left again into Cockspur Street, we come to the junction of Pall Mall and Haymarket. One east side of Haymarket once stood Her Majesty's Theatre. There have been a succession of theatres on the site. In *Nicholas Nickleby* the dastardly Sir Mulberry Hawk, with his acolytes, Pluck and Pyke, brought Mrs Nickleby to a box here. By prior arrangement, Kate Nickleby was brought to the adjacent box with the Witterleys. It was a humiliation of Kate.

Trafalgar Square to the north of Whitehall is where this walk ends – and where we started with Walk One.

The First Suburbs

1. Camden Town

The inner Ring Road from Paddington to Islington, made up today of Marylebone Road, Euston Road, Pentonville Road and City Road was a new road, built by order of an Act of Parliament in 1757, and was known as "The New Road" until 1857. It marked a line on the northern expansion of London, but not for long. Regent's Park was designed during the Napoleonic Wars and urban development crept north of the road during the first half of the nineteenth century. There was a decided class distinction south and north of the line. To the south were the aristocratic estates of Bloomsbury and what later became known as Fitzrovia. Only Clerkenwell was a more plebeian enclosure south of the New Road. To the north Somers Town was developed on land owned by Lord Somers between what is now Euston and King's Cross. Further north Camden Town grew up on land owned by Lord Camden. Somers Town and Camden Town – and Pentonville to the east – were residential areas for the burgeoning lower middle class that worked in the cities of Westminster and London.

These were districts of uncertain and changing social composition. Somers Town in the early part of the nineteenth century became a home for French and Spanish migrants. Terraced houses were smaller as you went north. Most people walked to their work, two, three or four miles each day. Public transport was limited and expensive, and only expanded and became cheaper after the middle of the century. Just as Dickens himself used to walk from Camden Town to Hungerford Stairs each morning, so Bob Cratchit in *A Christmas Carol* went from Camden Town to the City. During the rush hours of mornings and evenings the streets would have been thronged with pedestrians.

It was still semi-rural when the Dickens family moved into Bayham Street in 1823 from Chatham. A Veterinary College was founded in Camden Town in 1791 to improve animal husbandry. It specialised in dealing with cavalry horses during the Napoleonic Wars. The College still exists on Royal College Street and is now part of the University of London. North of Camden Town were the wooded uplands of Hampstead and Highgate.

In his childhood and early teens Charles Dickens had several homes in this area, thanks to the financially unstable nature of his family's finances. In 1823 the Dickens family lived at number 16 (later numbered 141) Bayham Street for a year. It was **a small mean tenement, with a wretched little back-garden abutting on a squalid court**. Demolished before the First World War, it had been built in about 1812 and was rented for £22 a year. The house had four rooms, a basement and a **little back-garret**, all quite cramped for the Dickens family that in 1823 included six children. The window frame from the little back-garret room that Charles Dickens occupied has been salvaged and can be seen at the Dickens Museum in Doughty Street. In his room Dickens had a toy theatre that he had brought from Chatham. There was a meadow at the back – **frowzy fields, and cow-houses, and dung-hills, and dust-heaps, and ditches, and gardens, and summer-houses, and carpet-beating grounds**. On arrival Dickens, aged eleven, did not go to school. **I degenerated into cleaning his boots of a morning, and my own; and making myself useful in the work of that little house; and looking after my younger brothers and sisters; and going on such poor errands as**

arose out of our poor way of living. A plaque marks the site of the house on the north-eastern part of the road.

Tommy Traddles in *David Copperfield* lived in this area **in a little street near the Veterinary College at Camden Town, which was principally tenanted, as one of the clerks who lived in that direction informed me, by gentlemen students, who bought live donkeys and made experiments on those quadrupeds in their private apartments ... The inhabitants appeared to have a propensity to throw any little trifles they were not in want of, into the road: which not only made it rank and sloppy, but untidy too, on account of the cabbage leaves. The refuse was not wholly vegetable either, for I myself saw a shoe, a doubled-up saucepan, a black bonnet, and an umbrella, in various stages of decomposition, as I was looking for the number I wanted.**

Bayham Street today has a few terraced houses that date from Dickens's time. A building to the south of Dickens's old home houses the main office of the Variety Club of Great Britain. This would have pleased Dickens. The Variety Club started in Pittsburgh, Pennsylvania, as a charity for sick, disabled or disadvantaged children, and is promoted by show business personalities. The British branch was launched in 1949. Their most visible activity is the fleet of Sunshine Coaches that take children and their families on outings to places of amusement and interest.

As a boy Dickens wandered all over the area, observing everything. His real world was circumscribed by poverty, humiliation, his father's debts and his own demeaning work in the blacking factory. His imaginative world was stimulated by the world of marginal London, newly arrived migrants from the countryside who lived on their wits and provided basic services – food, drink, clothes – to others also living on the margin. His observations were stored up to be recycled in his mature fiction.

Although the Bayham Road house was his main home in the

area, his family moved around and rented accommodation south
of the New Road in Gower Street, and in Somers Town. Other
temporary homes were in Johnson Street (now Cranleigh Street)
off Eversholt Street – **a charming little villa** – and in the Polygon,
an arrangement of houses in the form of a circle within Claren-
don Square. On Seymour Street (now Eversholt Street) stands St
Mary's Church, in the early nineteenth century known as Somers
Chapel, which Dickens occasionally attended. Johnson Street was
then at the northern fringe of Somers Town and was separated from
Camden Town by fields. In *Bleak House* Harold Skimpole had a dysfunctional family home in the Polygon. The older pattern of roads
here has disappeared and only Polygon Road survives as a reminder.
In Somers Town, Dickens noted, **there was at that time a number
of poor Spanish refugees walking about in cloaks, smoking little
paper cigars.** While his father was in the Marshalsea with the rest of
his family, the young Charles was a lodger in Little College Street, a
few roads to the east of Bayham Street with **a reduced old lady**, Mrs
Roylance, who became a model for Mrs Pipchin in *Dombey and Son*.

After a legacy allowed John Dickens to pay off his debts and
obtain release from the Marshalsea Charles was able to leave work
at the blacking factory and – joy of joys! – attend school. The school
chosen was Wellington House Academy in Hampstead Road, at the
junction of Granby Street (now Terrace) and Hampstead Road. The
whole configuration of streets, as well as many of their names, has
changed since the 1820s. Moreover the whole was turned upside
down with the building of the railway lines. No trace of the school
exists today. (But just north of Granby Terrace at 263 Hampstead
Road, on the wall of a faded house that has seen better days, a plaque
tells us that was once the home of George Cruikshank (1792–1878),
who did illustrations for *Sketches by Boz* and *Oliver Twist*.) Dickens
used the school as a model for Salem House in *David Copperfield*.
It was his only secondary schooling and he left when he was fifteen.

Education does not seem to have been taken very seriously. The pupils kept many pets. **Red-polls, linnets, and even canaries were kept in desks, drawers, hat-boxes and other strange refuges for birds; but white mice were the favourite stock. The boys trained the white mice much better than the masters trained the boys.**

In the twenty years after Dickens's schooldays in Hampstead Road the whole area was totally transformed, physically and socially, by the building of the railways from two termini – Euston and King's Cross. Two railway lines were built by two different railway companies, the London and Birmingham (from 1846 the London and North Western) and the Midland, to the Midlands and the north of England. There were geographical problems in driving the railway lines north. Already the areas immediately north of the two stations were being built up, and it would have been too expensive to buy the land and compensate the people who lived there. Anyway the hills of Hampstead and Highgate were in the way. Tunnels were very expensive and had to be avoided if possible. So the lines swing off to the west. Poorer (and, for the railway companies, cheaper) quarters were cleared and only one major tunnel, under Primrose Hill, was built.

In *Dombey and Son* Paul Dombey's nanny, Mrs Toodle, lived at Staggs's Gardens, Camden Town – or **Camberling Town** as the inhabitants called it. Staggs's Gardens cannot be located. It or its inspiration has probably been swept away with the railway developments. It was still semi-rural in the novel. Staggs's Gardens **was a little row of houses with squalid patches of ground before them, fenced off with old doors, barrel staves, scraps of tarpaulin, and dead bushes; with bottomless tin kettles, and exhausted iron fenders, thrust into the gaps. Here the Staggs's Gardeners trained scarlet beans, kept fowls and rabbits, erected rotten summer-houses, dried clothes, and smoked pipes.**

Mrs Toodle's husband worked for the railways and his language is full of railway imagery. He was constructing Primrose Hill tunnel, a thousand-metre tunnel between Chalk Farm and Swiss Cottage. In *Dombey and Son* Dickens has an apocalyptic description of the changes to the physical environment.

The first shock of a great earthquake had, just at that period, rent the whole neighbourhood to its centre. Traces of its course were visible on every side. Houses were knocked down, streets broken through and stopped, deep pits and trenches dug in the ground, enormous heaps of earth and clay thrown up, buildings that were undermined and shaken propped up with great beams of wood. Here a chaos of carts, overthrown and jumbled together, lay topsy-turvy at the bottom of a steep, unnatural hill; there, confused treasures of iron soaked and rusted in something that had accidentally become a pond. Everywhere were bridges that led nowhere, thoroughfares that were wholly impassable ... There were a hundred thousand shapes and substances of incompleteness wildly mingled out of their places, upside down, burrowing in the earth, aspiring in the air, mouldering in water, and unintelligible as any dream.

The railway, or **railroad**, as Dickens called it, is invisible today. It is in a deep trench alongside Hampstead Road with walls too high to see passing trains. Even passengers on those trains travelling north are unable to appreciate the magnificent entry into the Primrose Hill tunnel, designed in 1837 by Robert Stephenson.

2. Chelsea

In the 1830s Chelsea was a fishing village on the river Thames with its own identity separate from London. In the previous century it had been a dangerous place. In *Barnaby Rudge*, **few would venture ... to Chelsea, unarmed and unattended**. During the eighteenth century some smart houses were being built in the orchards to the north of the river. In 1838, in a letter to Leigh Hunt, Dickens could describe Chelsea as **in the country.** In the 1820s and 1830s it became a place that attracted artists and writers, people who wanted some detachment from the social whirl of the metropolis. Dickens located two of his secondary characters in Chelsea – Mr Bayham Badger, cousin of Mr Kenge, in *Bleak House*, and Miss Sophie Wackles, object of Dick Swiveller's passion, in *The Old Curiosity Shop.*

St Luke's Church was built in 1818–20 in an unselfconscious Gothic Revival style. Light and spacious, it catered for the smart new bourgeoisie who distanced themselves from the river folk around Chelsea Old Church. The first rector of St Luke's was a brother of the Duke of Wellington. The rector in 1836 was Charles Kingsley. The Old Church, where Sir (St) Thomas More is buried, was bombed in the Second World War and has been largely rebuilt, and so is "not older" than St Luke's. Henry James, the American-born novelist, died in Chelsea. His funeral was held at the Old Church in 1916. The cremation was at Golders Green and the ashes taken to Cambridge, Massachusetts. There is a memorial to James in the Old Church churchyard.

The family of Dickens's wife, Catherine Hogarth, lived at 18 York Place, to the south of Fulham Road. Her father, George, was a Scot and had known Sir Walter Scott. He had come to London in 1834 as music and dramatic critic of the *Morning Chronicle*, thereby becoming a colleague of Dickens. Hogarth and Dickens got on well together. Dickens was invited to the house where he met Catherine, one of several daughters, and fell in love. He was a regular visitor. He was always a practical joker. On one occasion, he himself recalled, **a young man dressed as a sailor jumped in at the window, danced a hornpipe, whistling the tune, jumped out again, and a few minutes later Charles Dickens walked gravely in at the door, as if nothing had happened, shook hands all round, and then, at the sight of their puzzled faces, burst into a roar of**

laughter. York Place has disappeared and the Royal Brompton Hospital occupies its site. Dickens's engagement lasted a year, and to be nearer his fiancée he rented for several months 11 Selwood Terrace nearby, a house in a recently built row of terrace houses, that were then surrounded by open country. (There is no plaque on the house; nor is there one on number 9, where D H Lawrence lodged before his marriage in 1914.) Dickens's finances were being stretched for he was already also paying rent on the flat in Furnival's Inn, Holborn.

Charles Dickens and Catherine Hogarth were married at St Luke's Church on 2 April 1836. Apart from members of the Hogarth and Dickens families the only others present were the best man, Thomas Beard, another parliamentary reporter and fellow-journalist, and John Macrone, a publisher who had bought the copyright of *Sketches by Boz*. Dickens's financial situation was about to be changed dramatically for the first number of *Pickwick Papers* appeared just two days before. The reception was at York Place, then confronting orchards and market gardens. The couple went off to Chalk near Rochester in Kent for their honeymoon.

Dickens walked all over London and in 1861 walked through Chelsea by the river. He set out from the offices of *All the Year Round* in Wellington Street North. **The day was so beautifully bright and warm that I thought I would walk on by Millbank, to see the river. I walked straight on for three miles on a splendid broad esplanade overhanging the Thames, with immense factories, railway works, and whatnot erected on it, and with the strangest beginnings and ends of wealthy streets pushing themselves into the very Thames. When I was a rower on that river, it was all broken ground and ditch, with here and there a public-house or two, an old mill, and a tall chimney. I had never seen it in any state of transition, though I suppose myself to know this rather large city as well as anyone in it.**

Half a mile to the south of St Luke's Church is Upper Cheyne

Row. On the north side at number 22 lived Leigh Hunt, the gifted, feckless dilettante. Dickens portrayed him as the gifted, feckless dilettante Harold Skimpole in *Bleak House*. Leigh Hunt did not recognise himself at first and when he did find out he was deeply upset.

Between Upper Cheyne Row and the river is Cheyne Row where, at number 24, the National Trust owns Carlyle's House, built in 1703. The Carlyles had known Leigh Hunt and visited him here in Chelsea. In Carlyle's view, Chelsea was "unfashionable; it was once the resort of the Court and great, however; hence numerous old houses in it, at once cheap and excellent." He saw the house in Cheyne Row, liked it and leased it at a rent of £35 a year. The Carlyles stayed there for the rest of their lives. Thomas Carlyle died here in 1881.

Carlyle was seventeen years older than Dickens who hero-worshipped him: **I would go at all times farther to see Carlyle than any man alive.** Dickens wrote to one of his sons that Carlyle was **the man who had influenced** him **most.** Carlyle had a respect and affection for the younger man, though he was suspicious of what he called "fictioneering". Carlyle was one of the select handful who came to listen to Dickens reading *The Chimes* in 1844 at John Forster's house in Lincoln's Inn Fields. Both men professed a tough radical humanitarianism. (In both men the toughness could manifest itself in a brutal racism.) Each developed a literary style of his own, a style that was creatively journalistic rather than traditionally literary. Both were outsiders, and Dickens owed much to Carlyle's *French Revolution* in his writing of *A Tale of Two Cities*. Indeed Carlyle helped him with the writing of the book and used to lend him a "cartload" of books from the London Library. Dickens was a frequent visitor to Carlyle's house. Dickens came to Cheyne Row and called on Carlyle. But there was never the reciprocal entertainment on the scale that Dickens hosted in his successive London homes. Carlyle was not, as his wife, Jane, was, extrovert. Nor was the house suitable for entertaining. In 1852 the Carlyles did extend one room on the first floor when the attic was adapted for use as Carlyle's study.

Mrs Carlyle died in 1866 and when Dickens died four years later, Carlyle was heartbroken: "No death since 1866 had fallen on me with such a stroke ... The good, the gentle ... noble Dickens – every inch of him an honest man."

The Chelsea Embankment was built in the 1870s. Gardens and a road flank the river. A statue of a seated and brooding Carlyle looks over the river. A few yards to the right is a statue of Sir Thomas More.

3. Greenwich

Greenwich was a separate town in the early nineteenth century, with a history of royal patronage and associations with the Royal Navy. In the early 1830s it had a population of about 25,000. Originally a fishing village, it became a favoured royal residence from the fifteenth century. Two of England's best-known monarchs, King Henry VIII and Queen Elizabeth I, were born here. The former monarch married two of his wives in Greenwich. King Henry VIII is also popularly seen as the founder of the Royal Navy and until the nineteenth century ships were built at nearby Woolwich and Deptford. King Charles II laid out Greenwich Park in the 1660s and, patron of scientific learning that he was, established the Royal Observatory there, through which the meridian line passes.

The town near the river and the pier is dominated by the royally sponsored buildings, Greenwich Hospital, the Royal Naval College and the Queen's House, designed in the early seventeenth century by Inigo Jones.

Dickens, born at Portsmouth and reared in Chatham, two other towns associated with the Royal Navy, felt at home in Greenwich. The vernacular architecture – the smart terraced housing built for navy personnel – would remind him of the other two towns.

The best approach to Greenwich from London is not by the railway first built in the 1830s and so making the town the earliest of the commuter suburbs. Nor by the congested roads. Not even by the Docklands Light railway that disgorges passengers near the *Cutty Sark*, the last of the tea clippers that sailed to the Far East in the nineteenth century. The best approach is by river. Boats regularly ply from Westminster Pier and call at Tower Pier. It is possible to see parts of London associated with Dickens's novels – the Temple, Southwark, the area of Jacob's Island, the Grapes Tavern at Limehouse – in a way that would have been more familiar to Dickens and his contemporaries.

Greenwich was a favourite place for holiday excursions for Londoners. From the eighteenth century a regular Greenwich Fair was held in the Park which lasted three days in May. It became a riotous event. Roads from London as well as the river were crowded with traffic.

In 1835, two years before the railway arrived, the twenty-three year-old Dickens wrote a report on his journey to the Fair. It became one of the *Sketches by Boz*: **We cannot conscientiously deny the charge of having once made the passage in a spring van accompanied by thirteen gentlemen, fourteen ladies, an unlimited number of children, and a barrel of beer; and we have a vague recollection of having, in later days, found ourself the eighth outside, on the top of a hackney coach, at something past four o' clock in the morning, with a rather confused idea of our own name, or place of residence. We have grown older since then, and quiet, and steady.** (His style of reportage matured too.)

Dickens loved it all. He noted people playing "Kiss in the Ring" and "Threading my Grandmother's Needle". But **the principal amusement is to drag young ladies up the steep hill which leads to the observatory, and then drag them down again, at the very top of their speed, greatly to the derangement of their curls and** bonnet-caps, and much to the edification of lookers-on from below. The fair was a periodical breaking out, we suppose; a sort of rash; a three days' fever which cools the blood for six months after. But the Regency riotousness also attracted righteous preachers who denounced the licentiousness of the fair. The citizens of Greenwich too were not keen on this annual invasion and campaigned to have it stopped. Nathaniel Hawthorne in the 1850s found the Fair "little more than a confusion of unwashed and shabbily dressed people ... . The common people of England," he went on to observe prissily, "have no daily familiarity with even so necessary a thing as a washbowl, not to mention a bathing-tub." Cleanliness and godliness finally triumphed and the last Fair was held in 1857.

Greenwich became celebrated also for its riverside taverns that provided whitebait allegedly from the Thames. Dickens himself used to patronise The Ship which was bombed in the Second World War. Its site is now occupied by the *Cutty Sark*. A party for Dickens was hosted for him here on his return from America in 1842, and another when *Martin Chuzzlewit* was published. In his last novel, *Our Mutual Friend*, Bella Wilfer and her father have dinner at The Ship, **overlooking the river ... looking at the ships and steamboats.** She later was married to John Rokesmith at the Greenwich Parish Church of St Alfege. The church has a history going back a thousand years, but the present building was designed by Nicholas Hawksmoor, also responsible for St Anne's Limehouse, St George's-in-the-East Shadwell and the western towers of Westminster Abbey. The church porch, **having swallowed up Bella Wilfer for ever and ever, had it not in its power to relinquish that young woman but slid into the happy sunlight Mrs John Rokesmith instead.** The newlyweds went on to have dinner at The Ship. **The marriage dinner was the crowning success, for what had bride and bridegroom plotted to do, but to have and hold that dinner in the very room of the hotel where Pa and the lovely woman had dined together! ... And** the dishes being seasoned with Bliss – an article which they are sometimes out of at Greenwich – were of perfect flavour, and the golden drinks had been bottled in the golden age and hoarding up their sparkles ever since.

Only one of the famous Greenwich riverside taverns has survived. The Trafalgar Tavern to the east of Greenwich Hospital is crowded and still serves whitebait. There is a classless buzz about the place, reminding one of a popular seaside resort. You have the benefit of piped music and on Wednesday nights there is "an evening of acoustic music, featuring musicians from Greenwich and beyond", perhaps the twenty-first century equivalent of the Greenwich Fair.

Mr and Mrs Rokesmith took **a modest little cottage, but bright and fresh** at Blackheath.

Blackheath is above Greenwich, and was on the old road to Rochester and Canterbury, **at the end of the long vista of gnarled old trees in Greenwich Park.** In *David Copperfield* Salem House, the school attended by David, Traddles and Steerforth and headed by Mr Creakle, was **down by Blackheath.** David, on his walk from London to Dover, sleeps rough for a night behind the school, **in a corner where there used to be a haystack. I imagined that it would be a kind of company to have the boys, and the bedroom where I used to tell the stories, so near to me.**

Beyond Blackheath, to the east, is Shooter's Hill, the location for the opening chapter of *A Tale of Two Cities,* when the Dover mail coach is stopped. The area was notorious for its highwaymen and when Jerry Cruncher stopped the coach, passengers and crew were much alarmed. The **guard suspected the passengers, the passengers suspected one another and the guard ... and the coachman was sure of nothing but the horses.** And Shooter's Hill is where Tony Weller finally retires in *Pickwick Papers,* taking a public house, **where he is quite reverenced as an oracle.**

4. Hampstead

The uplands of Hampstead and Highgate have retained the role that they have had for centuries. Near enough to the capital for convenience, far enough away to enjoy the open country. Hampstead, swathed and protected by the Heath, can still kid itself that it is a "village". It has always attracted residents who were artistically inclined or politically radical. It was the home for the Labour Party leaders, Hugh Gaitskell and Michael Foot.

Hampstead was important for Dickens. After the traumatic death of his sister-in-law, Mary Hogarth, in 1837, while he was writing simultaneously *Pickwick Papers* and *Oliver Twist*, he retreated to a Hampstead farmhouse, Wyldes Farm. This is located just off Hampstead Way. The farmer used to occupy a converted barn and to let out the farmhouse – often to artists and writers. But Dickens did not acquire that familiarity for the place and people which he had for the parts of London nearer the centre. Hampstead was a place of retreat and recreation. It was a favourite resort for Dickens who would persuade friends to ride a horse out there energetically to the public house, Jack Straw's Castle. **I knows a good 'ouse there**, he wrote to John Forster, **when we can have a red-hot chop for dinner and a glass of wine**.

Washington Irving commemorated the inn in his *Tales of a Traveller*, and Thackeray and the painter, Lord Leighton, were later regulars. Jack Straw's Castle has had its present name only for two centuries, before when it was known just as "the castle". The fourteenth-century leader of the Peasants' Revolt is alleged to have sought refuge in the area. Jack Straw's Castle is no longer a pub, but a "personal training club", whatever that means. The present building is of no great antiquity. It was destroyed in the Second World War and rebuilt in the 1960s in what has been described as Georgian Gothick. In the nineteenth century John Sadleir, a financier and swindler, committed suicide behind Jack Straw's Castle.

The **immensely rich** Mr Merdle MP in *Little Dorrit* was based on Sadleir.

A mile to the east, also on the edge of the Heath is Spaniard's Inn, an eighteenth-century construction. It is still a pub. In the eighteenth century some of the Gordon Rioters were detained there, diverted from the sacking of Kenwood (then Caen Wood), the home of the liberal lawyer, Lord Mansfield, as described in *Barnaby Rudge*. And in *Pickwick Papers* Mrs Bardell had tea here with her son and some friends before being lured into custody by an employee of the solicitors, Dodson and Fogg, to be detained at the Fleet prison.

David Copperfield used to stride out to Hampstead. Dick Swiveller in *The Old Curiosity Shop* had a cottage **which had in the garden a smoking-box, the envy of the civilised world.**

Bill Sikes, after the murder of Nancy in *Oliver Twist* wanders around Hampstead Heath near Kenwood. Like Dick Whittington four centuries earlier he went to Highgate and turned back but, **unsteady of purpose and uncertain where to go, struck off to the right again almost as soon as he began to descend it, and taking the footpath across the fields that skirted Caen Wood, and so came out on Hampstead Heath. Traversing the hollow by the Vale of Health, he mounted the opposite bank, and crossing the road which joins the villages of Hampstead and Highgate, made along the remaining portion of the Heath to the fields at North End.** He continued to wander – to Hendon and Hatfield before he returned to central London and eventual death in Bermondsey.

5. Highgate

Highgate has many of the qualities of Hampstead, and with, if anything, more literary associations. There was no parish church until the nineteenth century, and the chapel at Highgate School was used for Anglican worship. Dickens lived here briefly in 1832 at 92

North Road – a plaque is on the wall. In the same road the poet A E Housman (1859–1936) had a house and the former Poet Laureate, John Betjeman (1906–84), went to school.

The parish church of St Michael was being built while Dickens was in North Road. Opposite the church at 3 The Grove is a house with two plaques noting earlier literary occupiers – Samuel Taylor Coleridge (1772–1834), author of "The Ancient Mariner" and the twentieth century novelist, journalist and broadcaster, J B Priestley (1894–1984).

St Michael's Church looks down on the extensive Highgate Cemetery on both sides of Swain's Lane. The eastern cemetery hosts the graves of Karl Marx and Dickens's novelist contemporary, George Eliot. The more extensive western cemetery has the graves of Dickens's parents, Elizabeth and John Dickens. He wrote the epitaph for his father, describing him as a **zealous, useful, cheerful spirit**. Also buried in the family grave is his daughter, Dora, darkly named after the wife of David Copperfield – he was writing this at the time. The real Dora died as an infant the following year.

Between St Michael's Church and the Highgate Literary and Scientific Institution is Church House, 10 South Grove. This is reckoned to be the home of David Copperfield's overbearing and amoral school friend, James Steerforth. In the same novel, Dr Strong, the old Canterbury teacher and scholar, retired with his daughter, Annie, to Highgate – precise location unknown – and David and Dora had their marital home next door, accommodating also Betsey Trotwood and Mr Dick.

As with Hampstead, Dickens never *internalised* Highgate. It is a retreat from the city for his characters, outsiders who settle there. Similarly it is a place of transit for other characters. Noah Claypole and Charlotte in *Oliver Twist* pass under Highgate Archway on their way to the city of London. It is at the Archway that Inspector Bucket picks up the trail of the fugitive Lady Dedlock in *Bleak*

House, and in *Barnaby Rudge* Joe Willett, after saying farewell to Dolly Varden, wanders up to Highgate to meditate **but there were no voices in the bells to bid him turn.**

6. Limehouse

Until the nineteenth century, the "East End" of London immediately north of the river Thames, to the east of the Tower of London, consisted of a string of villages – Wapping, Shadwell, Limehouse and Ratcliffe – surrounded by marshy land and market gardens. There was a tradition of sea-faring and boat-building among the village menfolk going back to the early sixteenth century. It became an area of migration from overseas in the nineteenth century. In the first decade of the century the East and West India Docks were built and a private company constructed the Commercial Road to facilitate the bringing of goods from the new docks to central London. These were followed in the next half century with a chain of docks, along with vast warehouses and offices. All were contained behind grim brick walls. One of the last, the Royal Victoria Dock, begun in 1850, covered 94 acres of water and was then the largest such dock in the world. North and south of the river there are swing bridges on canals that lead from the river to the docks. **Captain Cuttle,** in *Dombey and Son*, lived at Limehouse **on the brink of a little canal near the India Docks, where there was a swivel bridge which opened now and then to let in some wandering monster of a ship come roaming up the street like a stranded leviathan.**

The east end of the City, around Bevis Marks synagogue, was already a Jewish (mainly Sephardic) quarter. From 1850 and increasingly after the 1870s, Jews, mostly Ashkenazi, migrated here from central and eastern Europe, creating the Jewish East End. During the nineteenth century communities of Chinese and of Lascars, a generic term for sailors from the lands bordering the Indian Ocean, settled here. And during the same period the villages were absorbed into the expanding urbanisation of London. In the last hundred years it became peopled by later immigrants. Today Bengali has replaced Yiddish as the language of the streets and the Chinese cultural contribution has been take-away restaurants rather than opium dens. But an aroma of curry pervades Cable Street, which marks a social and ethnic frontier. To the north is international Limehouse. To the south as far as the river Thames is another world. Warehouses have been converted to flats and offices. This is a world of global capitalism, an extension from Wapping and Canary Wharf.

Dickens, with a father who worked for the Naval Pay Board, with Portsmouth as a birthplace and with happy childhood memories of Chatham, had a particular affection for sailors and people connected with the sea. Though some may be eccentric, none of his villainous characters is associated with the sea. In his childhood he called on his godfather, Christopher Huffam, a ship's chandler, who lived at Church Row, now Newell Street, perhaps in one of the handful of eighteenth-century terraced houses that run south-west of the splendid early eighteenth-century church of St Anne, designed by Nicholas Hawksmoor. These are all that are left to suggest even to the most sensitive social archaeologist that here was once a village centre.

Dickens's visits to Limehouse may have be recreated in *Dombey and Son*, when Walter Gay went to see Captain Cuttle in Limehouse past **slopsellers' shops ... anchor and chain-cable forges ... rows of houses, with little vane-surmounted masts uprearing themselves from among the scarlet beans. Then, ditches. Then, pollarded willows. Then, more ditches ... Then, the air was perfumed with chips, and all other trades were swallowed up in mast, oar, and block making, and boat building**. Captain Cuttle may have been modelled on Christopher Huffam.

Lizzie Hexham in *Our Mutual Friend* lived in Limehouse. **The low building had the look of having once been a mill. There was a rotten wart of wood upon its forehead that seemed to indicate where the sails had been.**

If we continue south along Newell Street and turn right into Three Colt Street we reach the eastern end of Narrow Street. All around are sanitised warehouses and former wharves have been converted into marinas. On the left at number 76, opposite Rope-makers Fields, is the Grapes Public House, generally accepted as the original for the Six Jolly Fellowship Porters tavern in *Our Mutual Friend*. Dickens described it as being **like a handle of a flat iron set upright on its broadest end.** (This was an image Dickens also used to describe his old school in Hampstead.) **It had long settled down into a state of hale infirmity. In its whole constitution it had not a straight floor, and hardly a straight line; but it had outlasted, and clearly would yet outlast, many a better-trimmed building, many a sprucer public-house. Externally it was a narrow, lopsided wooden jumble of corpulent windows heaped one upon another as you might heap as many toppling oranges, with a crazy wooden verandah impending over the water; indeed, the whole house, inclusive of the complaining flag-staff on the roof, impended over the water, but seemed to have got into the condition of a faint-hearted diver who has passed so long on the brink that he will never go in at all.** Today the pub is recognisable from Dickens's description. Framed pictures of Bill Sikes and Mr Pickwick – neither of whom had connections with the Six Jolly Fellowship Porters – adorn the walls, and peppermint and camomile tea is available in the bar. A pricey restaurant is upstairs, specialising in fish described – what a relief! – as fresh, but booking is recommended. The clientele is largely prosperous, white and European. The pub is best seen from the river.

One mile to the west, south-east of Shadwell station, are the Blue

Gate Fields schools. In the 1860s one of the most celebrated Chinese opium dens was located here, described as "a model of respectability" even though it was surrounded by brothels. In the company of his American friends, James T and Annie Adam Fields, Dickens visited an opium den here. He used the experience in the opening chapter of *The Mystery of Edwin Drood*.

Acknowledgements

I first became addicted to the writings of Charles Dickens when I was given a copy of *Oliver Twist* at the age of nine. I was encouraged in my addiction by my parents, Kenneth and Kitty Clark, and also my grandfather, William Clark, who left school when he was thirteen but knew his Dickens well; I remember him quoting *Bleak House* at my grandparents' golden wedding in 1954. In the mid-1960s I was at the University of Leicester and was inspired by the lectures and conversation of the great Dickens scholar, Philip Collins. In the 1970s I read several of Dickens's novels aloud to my first wife, Isobel.

In the writing of this book I have benefited from advice, ideas, information and the loan of books from many people, in particular Theresa Clark, John Peverley, Eve Smith, Sean Magee, Kat Whone, and Fernando at the George and Vulture Inn.

Bibliography

Dickens's works

I have used as my reading and working editions the Penguin Classics. There have been several editions, with different editors. I have worked on the latest available. I have also used other editions of other works, such as *Reprinted Pieces* and *Master Humphrey's Clock*, *The Christmas Stories* and *The Uncommercial Traveller*. The Penguin Classics editions are as follows, in chronological order of composition, with the original date of publication in brackets after the title, with the editor of the volume in the series named after the title.

Sketches by Boz (1839), Dennis Walder, 1995
The Pickwick Papers (1836–37), Mark Womald, 1999
Oliver Twist (1837–38), Philip Horne, 2002
Nicholas Nickleby (1839), Mark Ford, 1999
The Old Curiosity Shop (1841), Norman Page, 2000
Barnaby Rudge (1841), John Bowen, 2003
A Christmas Carol and Other Christmas Writings (1835–54),
    Michael Slater, 2003
Martin Chuzzlewit (1843–44), Patricia Ingham, 2004
Dombey and Son (1848), Andrew Sanders, 2002
David Copperfield (1850), Jeremy Tambling, 2004
Bleak House (1853), Nicola Bradbury, 1996
Hard Times (1854), Kate Flint, 2003

Little Dorrit (1857), Stephen Wall, 1998, and Helen Small, 2003
A Tale of Two Cities (1859), Richard Maxwell, 2003
Great Expectations (1860–61), David Trotter and Charlotte
    Mitchell, 1996
Our Mutual Friend (1865), Adrian Poole, 1997
The Mystery of Edwin Drood (1870), David Paroissien, 2002
Selected Journalism 1850–1870, David Pascoe, 1997
Selected Short Fiction, Deborah A Thomas, 1976
I have also consulted the Pilgrim Edition of the Letters of Charles
Dickens, edited by Madeline House, Graham Storey and Kathleen
Tillotson, 12 volumes, Oxford University Press, 1965–2002.

Other works

Ackroyd, Peter, *Dickens*, Sinclair Stevenson, London, 1990
Addison, William, *In the Steps of Charles Dickens*, Rich and
    Cowan, London, 1955
Allbut, Robert, *Rambles in Dickensland*, Chapman and Hall,
    London, c1902
Allen, Tudor, *Little Italy, The Story of London's Italian Quarter*,
    Camden Local Studies and Archive Centre, London, 2008
Aslet, Clive, *The Story of Greenwich*, Fourth Estate, London, 1999
Bacon, George, *Ordnance Atlas of London and Suburbs*, Harry
    Margary, London, 1987 (first published, 1888)
Boast, Mary, *The Story of Bermondsey*, The London Borough of
    Southwark, London, 2003 (first published, 1978)
Bradley, Simon and Nikolaus Pevsner, *The Buildings of England,
    London 6: Westminster*, Yale University Press, New Haven and
    London, 2005 (first published, 2003)
Cherry, Bridget and Nikolaus Pevsner, *The Buildings of England.
    London 4: North*, London, 1999 (first published, 1998)

Chesterton, G K, *Charles Dickens*, Methuen, London, 1928 (first published, 1906)

Cowper, Francis, *A Prospect of Gray's Inn*, (second edition), Graya, London, 1985 (first published, 1951)

Daniell, Timothy, *"Inns of Court"*, Wildy and Sons, London, 1985 (first published, 1971)

Denford, Steven, and F Peter Woodford, *Streets of Camden Town*, Camden History Society, London, 2003

Dickens, Mamie, *My father as I Recall Him*, The Roxburghe Press, Westminster, 1897

Fitzgerald, Percy, *Bozland, Dickens' Places and People*, Downey and Co, London, 1895

Forster, John, *Life of Charles Dickens* (3 vols), Chapman and Hall, London, 1872–74

Hardwick, Michael and Mollie Hardwick, *The Charles Dickens Encyclopedia*, Futura Publications, 1976 (first published, 1973)

Herber, Mark, *Legal London, A Pictorial History*, Phillimore, Chichester, 2007 (first published, 1999)

Hibbert, Christopher, *The Making of Charles Dickens*, Book Club Associates, London, 1967

Holdsworth, William S, *Charles Dickens as a Legal Historian*, Yale University Press, New Haven, 1928

House, Humphry, *The Dickens World*, Oxford University Press, London, 1941

Hughes, William R, *A Week's Tramp in Dickens-land*, Chapman and Hall, London, 1891

Hyde, Ralph (ed), *The A to Z of Georgian London*, London Topographical Society, London, 1982

Jackson, T A, *Charles Dickens: The Progress of a Radical*, Lawrence and Wishart, 1937

Kent, William, *London for Dickens Lovers*, Methuen, London, 1935

Kitton, Frederick G, *The Dickens Country*, Adam and Charles
Black, London, 1911 (first published 1905)

Mankowitz, Wolf, *Dickens of London*, Macmillan, New York, 1977
(first published, 1976)

Matz, B W, *Dickensian Inns and Taverns*, Cecil Palmer, London,
1923

Matz, B W, *The Inns and Taverns of "Pickwick"*, Cecil Palmer,
London, 1922 (first published, 1921)

Megarry, Robert, *An Introduction to Lincoln's Inn*, The Honourable
Society of Lincoln's Inn, London, 2007

Newton, Douglas, *London west of the Bars*, Robert Hale, London,
1951

Paterson, Michael, *Inside Dickens' London*, David and Charles,
Newton Abbot, 2011

Picard, Liza, *Victorian London*, Phoenix, London, 2005

Prettejohns, Graham and others, *Charles Dickens and Southwark.*
The London Borough of Southwark, London, 1994 (first
published, 1974)

Prothero, Rowland E, *The Life and Correspondence of Arthur
Penrhyn Stanley DD*, 2 vols, John Murray, London, 1894

Rimmer, Albert, *About England with Dickens*, Chatto and
Windus, 1883

Sanders, Andrew, *Charles Dickens's London*, Robert Hale, London,
2010

Scholer, K A, *The Railways of Camden*, Camden History Society,
London, 2002

Slater, Michael, *Charles Dickens*, Yale University Press, New Haven
and London, 2009

Stone, Richard, *Gray's Inn, A Short History*, The Masters of the
Bench, London, 1997

Summerson, John, *Georgian London*, Penguin Books,
Harmondsworth, 1962 (first published, 1945)

Weinreb, Ben and others, *The London Encyclopaedia*, Macmillan, London, 2010 (first published, 1983)

White, Jerry, *London in the 19th Century*, Vintage Books, London, 2008 (first published, 2007)

Index